Cambridge Elements

Elements in Indigenous Environmental Research
edited by
Dina Gilio-Whitaker
California State University San Marcos
Clint Carroll
University of Colorado Boulder
Joy Porter
University of Birmingham

Associate Editor
Matthias Wong
National University of Singapore

THE REDISCOVERY OF HUACA PINTADA

Why Traditional Ecological Knowledge Matters Within Archaeological Environments in Peru

Sâm Ghavami
University of Fribourg

Christian Cancho Ruiz
University of Virginia

Shaftesbury Road, Cambridge CB2 8EA, United Kingdom

One Liberty Plaza, 20th Floor, New York, NY 10006, USA

477 Williamstown Road, Port Melbourne, VIC 3207, Australia

314–321, 3rd Floor, Plot 3, Splendor Forum, Jasola District Centre, New Delhi – 110025, India

Cambridge University Press is part of Cambridge University Press & Assessment, a department of the University of Cambridge.

We share the University's mission to contribute to society through the pursuit of education, learning and research at the highest international levels of excellence.

www.cambridge.org
Information on this title: www.cambridge.org/9781009583718

DOI: 10.1017/9781009583732

© Sâm Ghavami and Christian Cancho Ruiz 2026

This publication is in copyright. Subject to statutory exception and to the provisions of relevant collective licensing agreements, no reproduction of any part may take place without the written permission of Cambridge University Press & Assessment.

When citing this work, please include a reference to the DOI 10.1017/9781009583732

First published 2026

A catalogue record for this publication is available from the British Library

ISBN 978-1-009-58371-8 Hardback
ISBN 978-1-009-58370-1 Paperback
ISSN 2755-0826 (online)
ISSN 2755-0818 (print)

Cambridge University Press & Assessment has no responsibility for the persistence or accuracy of URLs for external or third-party internet websites referred to in this publication and does not guarantee that any content on such websites is, or will remain, accurate or appropriate.

For EU product safety concerns, contact us at Calle de José Abascal, 56, 1°, 28003 Madrid, Spain, or email eugpsr@cambridge.org

The Rediscovery of Huaca Pintada

Why Traditional Ecological Knowledge Matters Within Archaeological Environments in Peru

Elements in Indigenous Environmental Research

DOI: 10.1017/9781009583732
First published online: January 2026

Sâm Ghavami
University of Fribourg

Christian Cancho Ruiz
University of Virginia

Author for correspondence: Sâm Ghavami, sam.ghavami@unifr.ch

Abstract: This Element presents a case study of the authors' partnership with the La Pintada community in their excavation of a pre-Columbian site known as Huaca Pintada, a pyramidal mound located in the Lambayeque region on the north coast of Peru. The site, which gained recognition after the fortuitous discovery by looters in 1916 of an exceptional polychrome mural, was somehow "forgotten" by the scientific community after irreversible damage. However, this was not the case for the local inhabitants, families like the Inoñán or the Chapoñán descendants of ancient muchic traditions, who founded a village named after their illustrious elder. This Element describes how local actors like shamans and workers were indispensable in finding solutions that led not only to the rediscovery of the treasures of the Huaca Pintada but also to the reconnection of the community with its past.

Keywords: Andean archaeology, mural paintings, traditional ecological knowledge in Peru, Lambayeque, collaborative archaeology

© Sâm Ghavami and Christian Cancho Ruiz 2026

ISBNs: 9781009583718 (HB), 9781009583701 (PB), 9781009583732 (OC)
ISSNs: 2755-0826 (online), 2755-0818 (print)

Contents

1 Navigating Tensions: Integrating Indigenous Knowledge and Ownership in Peruvian Archaeology — 1

2 The Huaca Pintada Archaeological Project — 4

3 Archaeology, Conservation, and Preservation of Huaca Pintada — 35

4 Archaeological Sites as Indigenous Anchors in the Landscape — 58

5 Conclusions — 65

References — 68

1 Navigating Tensions: Integrating Indigenous Knowledge and Ownership in Peruvian Archaeology

The discipline of archaeology seeks to understand past events and the origins of human societies' customs. The materiality it studies, composed of ancient artifacts, abandoned structures, and the landscapes related to them, provides a glimpse into the complexity of human development throughout history. However, in recent decades, the validity of predominant models in the Western academic tradition – which emphasize empirical data, scientific objectivity, and universalist interpretations – has increasingly been questioned (Shanks and Tilley, 2016). This shift has introduced significant challenges, such as reconciling archaeological research with local perspectives and traditional ecological knowledge, that prioritize a more contextual understanding and foregrounds affective and relational connections to the past (Atalay, 2010; Jessen *et al.*, 2022; Smith, 1999; Wobst, 2010). The Peruvian context vividly highlights these profound tensions, as conflicts between state legislation and Indigenous communities over territorial rights are frequent (Morales, 2024). These disputes are further complicated by the contentious issue of the ownership of pre-Columbian remains, which hinders archaeological work and creates a highly intricate landscape for heritage exploration (Cojti Ren, 2010). Addressing these difficulties requires a paradigm shift that recenters Indigenous voices and values in archaeological practice. In this Element, we argue why the Peruvian case can become a model for more equitable and inclusive approaches to heritage management.

By directly studying the remnants of the past, archaeologists have the power to create discourses that impact society, influencing our view of history. It is worth asking whether these narratives include the local voices whose interests are usually marginalized. This is relevant considering that many Indigenous communities surviving today have strong ties to the lands of their ancestors and maintain many traditional customs passed down through generations (Atalay, 2010, p. 84). These ancestral epistemologies therefore encompass intimate understandings of their environment in connection with a spiritual world still active in modern times. That is, they feature the complex relationships between land, resources, and spirituality expressed in daily cultural practices (Allen, 2021). While the passage of time and the impacts of colonialism and modernity on Indigenous communities are undeniable, it is still possible to find in Peru certain continuities and resistances that provide context for the analysis of pre-Columbian remains challenging our Western preconceptions (Atalay, 2010, p. 85).

On the other hand, it is true that many studies do not seek to create links with the communities living near archaeological sites beyond employing them for excavations. The reasons for this include colonial legacies prioritizing Western scientific methods, language barriers, and structural inequities marginalizing Indigenous voices in decision-making. As a result, archaeology risks perpetuating the same patterns of exclusion it often seeks to critique. In this sense, the multiple efforts to address these issues increasingly demonstrate global interest in initiatives like collaborative archaeology, which seeks to involve different members of Indigenous communities as active partners in research (Wobst, 2010, p. 23). Collaborative archaeology bridges the typical requirements of academic research and the reconsideration of the central role Indigenous communities play in conceiving their own history.

Decolonial and Indigenous studies imply that researchers reflect on their methodologies to redefine them and thus to be able to challenge the hegemonic discourses we still rely on (Smith, 1999). This attitude contributes to fostering a more just and mutually beneficial knowledge exchange where the local voice can also be heard. In this specific case, the validation of Indigenous communities to access and study the site transcends purely legal frameworks toward moral and ethical ones.

To address this point, we have opted to use a more literary and subjective writing style when telling the story of the members of the Huaca Pintada community. This decision can be fully justified within the framework of an approach to Indigenous studies, which vindicates an epistemological position questioning traditional modes of knowledge production, often rooted in Eurocentric paradigms (Shanks and Tilley, 2016; Smith, 1999). In other words, our goal is to create coherence between content and form. From this perspective, the use of a more sensitive and open style, inspired by literary or journalistic writings, attempts to go beyond the rigid objectification typical of classical scientific discourse. The latter, although indispensable in many fields, can reduce individuals and communities to mere data elements or objects of study. We believe that adopting a more subjective writing style allows for greater respect toward the actors themselves, recognizing the legitimacy of their stories and perspectives. This implies establishing proximity between the author and the study subjects, not to erase scientific rigor, but to reveal their humanity or character more subtly. This choice also reflects the wishes of the members of the La Pintada community, who expressed their desire to see their full names and parts of their personal stories included in the text when they read it. Thus this style of writing, midway between testimony and analysis, promotes a truer and more equitable understanding of their life and the experiences we shared in the field.

Yet in Latin American countries like Peru, the challenge of reconciling Indigenous perspectives seems even more complex due to the complicated interactions between the Indigenous peoples and strict state laws seeking to protect cultural sites and local communities (Anaya, 2014; Kania, 2019). The problem arises when these laws clash with the immediate needs of Indigenous communities living in areas surrounding archaeological sites. Peru's legal framework for cultural heritage protection, including the 2004 General Law of Cultural Heritage, prioritizes the preservation of archaeological sites as national assets. Although well intentioned, these laws often conflict with the rights and livelihoods of Indigenous communities living near or atop such sites. In many cases, state-led conservation projects impose land-use restrictions, such as prohibiting farming, construction, or grazing, essential for local subsistence. An illustrative case is the ongoing tension between the Peruvian government and Indigenous communities in the Sacred Valley of the Incas, home to iconic sites like Machu Picchu and Ollantaytambo (Doughty, 2014). While these sites are celebrated as symbols of national identity and attract millions of tourists annually, the surrounding communities often bear the burden of conservation policies. Farmers may be evicted or face fines for cultivating ancestral lands designated as protected areas, even though their agricultural practices are often sustainable and deeply rooted in the region's history.

Moreover, many sites are threatened by the illegal appropriation of territory by unscrupulous organizations that, through their actions, not only loot the remains but also destroy all contextual information related to cultural assets (Chirinos Ogata, 2018; Rødal, 2017; SAFE, 2018). Indigenous communities are frequently caught between conflicting imperatives: preserving cultural heritage, protecting their land from exploitation, and meeting their immediate economic needs. This tension underscores the insufficiency of state-centered conservation models that do not consider local realities. This dichotomy between total heritage preservation and meeting contemporary Indigenous communities' demands outlines a landscape of struggle for the recognition of rights, resource management, and the Indigenous peoples' identity (Cojti Ren, 2010, p. 203).

This issue also raises a question: Who has the right to claim and interpret pre-Columbian remains? The Peruvian state asserts its sovereignty over these sites as part of the national heritage, a stance rooted in postcolonial efforts to build a cohesive national identity.[1] However, this position often overlooks the fact that many archaeological sites hold specific significance for Indigenous

---

[1] Ownership disputes are also complicated by the role of international stakeholders. Museums, private collectors, and foreign archaeologists have historically removed artifacts from Peru, often under dubious circumstances. Although repatriation efforts, such as the return of Machu Picchu artifacts from Yale University, have gained traction in recent years, the broader legacy of colonial plunder continues to cast a shadow over archaeological practice (Swanson, 2009). Indigenous communities argue that these artifacts should not only be returned but also placed under local stewardship, challenging the state's monopoly over cultural heritage.

communities, who may see themselves as direct descendants and guardians of the cultures that created them. For example, the Nazca Lines, a UNESCO World Heritage site, are often framed in global discourse as an enigmatic marvel of human ingenuity. However, for local Indigenous groups, the geoglyphs are more than a tourist attraction or an object of scientific study; they are imbued with spiritual and cultural meaning. Similarly, the fortress of Kuélap in northern Peru, a pre-Inca structure built by the Chachapoya people, holds deep ancestral significance for contemporary Indigenous communities in the region. These groups may view state-led archaeological interventions as acts of dispossession, stripping them of their cultural agency and alienating them from their heritage.

In this context, the ambiguity surrounding pre-Columbian remains plays a crucial role in how the archaeological site is approached. Our case study, at the Huaca Pintada site located in the Lambayeque department on Peru's north coast, highlights the challenges faced during the site's excavation. A conflict arose because the monument was legally situated on private land belonging to a local family initially opposed to the project. However, we explore how solutions were achieved thanks to community support, which saw in the archaeological project a potential to reconnect with their ancestral legacy. Finally, we demonstrate how an approach based on mutual respect and reciprocity allowed access to the site and led to the rediscovery of the forgotten treasures of Huaca Pintada. In this way, the *huacas* served as a bridge, fostering integration between the archaeological project and the community. The term *huaca* (from Quechua, often translated as "sacred place" or "sacred object") designates natural formations or human-made monuments imbued with spiritual essence and agency within Andean cosmology.

Through our experience at the Huaca Pintada site, we aim to show that participation and collaboration with the Indigenous community emerged as key to addressing these challenges. Adopting community-based approaches in archaeology, such as participatory research and collaborative decision-making, establishes a solid foundation for mutual understanding, respect, and co-ownership of the archaeological heritage. Working together enables archaeologists and Indigenous communities to develop research agendas that honor Indigenous knowledge, respect cultural protocols, and empower local communities.

2 The Huaca Pintada Archaeological Project

2.1 The Historical and Cultural Contexts of Huaca Pintada

During the 9th century AD, more than 600 years before the European conquest of the continent, the Pacific coast of northern Peru experienced a significant cultural transformation following the decline of the Moche civilization. The Moche, who had thrived in this arid region since the beginning of the millennium, were renowned for their artistic refinement and monumental adobe temples, near which some of the wealthiest burials in South America have been discovered (Alva, 1994; Alva and Donnan, 1993; Castillo, 2001; Larco, 1948; Millaire, 2002). The resulting transitional period brought profound changes exacerbated by political, economic, and social disruption. As a result, the once great centers of Moche power were largely abandoned, giving way to major political restructuring that may have been catalyzed by migratory movements (Bawden, 1996; Rucabado-Yong, 2006; Rucabado-Yong and Castillo, 2003; Shimada, 1994). It is within this dynamic and tumultuous context that the Lambayeque culture emerged. Indeed, recent archaeological evidence suggests that this cultural development was part of a complex and highly dynamic social process, challenging previous assumptions about its origins (Castillo, 2012; Curo Chambergo and Rosas Fernández, 2014; Ghavami, 2021; Rucabado-Yong, 2006; Rucabado-Yong and Castillo, 2003). The Lambayeque or Sicán culture was largely influenced by the Moche cultural heritage, yet it also incorporated new elements and certain innovations from neighboring Andean cultures such as the Huari and the Cajamarca. This demonstrates how societies can reinterpret and transform elements of their past while adapting to new social and environmental realities. The resulting cultural expression is a testament to the resilience and creativity of these communities, producing a unique and rich cultural legacy (Lavalle, 1989; Makowski, 2016; Shimada, 1995; Wester La Torre, 2010).

The desert landscape of the northern coast of Peru remains deeply marked by its history. In the Lambayeque region alone, several hundred ancient pre-Columbian temples, shaped like truncated pyramids and known as huacas, still stand today. These structures carry an almost mystical aura, serving as a reminder that this region was once the sacred heartland of ancient civilizations. However, the environment has undergone significant changes over time. The huacas no longer occupy a central role in the political and religious life of the contemporary inhabitants of the north coast – at least not at first glance. This is because nearly half a millennium ago, the Spanish Crown imposed Catholicism on the subject peoples, and those who sought to revive the ancient beliefs were persecuted for idolatry (Gareis, 2007). Consequently, the huacas were abandoned, allowing time to exert its power of oblivion.

Today, the preservation of these ruins varies widely. Many are buried under layers of earth formed by natural sedimentation and wind. The most monumental structures remain prominent in the landscape, standing as enduring witnesses to the grandeur of the past. In contrast, the more modest huacas are often indistinguishable from ordinary mounds of earth to the untrained eye. It is

Fig. 1 Huaca El Pueblo in the center of the village of Túcume.

frequently the violent El Niño phenomena, which inundate the region every decade, that reveal their hidden structures through gaping cracks exposing the ancient mud bricks. Some huacas are now surrounded by cultivated fields, while others stand incongruously near gas stations or agricultural factories, far removed from the reverence they once commanded (Fig. 1).

2.2 An Enigmatic Pre-Columbian Fresco

Just one kilometer north of the village of Túcume, known for its immense archaeological site made up of 26 truncated pyramids (Heyerdahl *et al.*, 1995), a blue sign from the Ministry of Culture of Peru reads in capital letters "SITIO ARQUEOLOGICO LA PINTADA. ZONA ARQUEOLOGICA INTANGIBLE" (Fig. 2). The name of this huaca is familiar to archaeologists and other scholars who have studied this singular transitional phase even though before our work no major scientific excavation had ever been undertaken on the site. American pioneer Wendel Bennett intervened in Huaca Pintada during his research in northern Peru in 1936 but excavated only three small pits where he exhumed the remains of an individual belonging to the Lambayeque culture (Bennett, 1939). Then, in 1978, an article by American scholar Richard Schaedel reignited interest in this site, long neglected by the scientific community. Schaedel's work unveiled the iconography of a mysterious polychrome

Fig. 2 The sign from the Ministry of Culture of Peru signaling the Huaca Pintada.

mural, nearly 18 meters long, which had been accidentally discovered by a group of grave looters in 1916 (Schaedel, 1978).

This discovery was probably one of the most sensational of its time since in 1916 – only five years after Hiram Bingham's "international discovery" of Machu Picchu – little was known about the pre-Hispanic societies of the north coast of Peru. Naturally, the Spanish and mestizo chroniclers wrote extensively about the Incas, largely because this civilization had established a vast empire spanning 2,500,000 square kilometers along the Andes shortly before the arrival of the colonizers. We now know that the Inca Empire ruled for about a century between the 15th and 16th centuries and was the heir to a civilizational development spanning 4,000 years (Bauer, 1998; Kosiba, 2015; Pease, 2007). However, because no writing systems from these cultures have been deciphered, the traces left behind – primarily archaeological remains – are essential to understanding their history. By uncovering these remnants buried in the earth, we can learn about the peoples who inhabited these regions before the rise of the Incas. Representations of daily life and religious practices offer invaluable opportunities to interpret their meaning and reconstruct the customs of these ancient societies. To achieve this, it is necessary to study their symbols and way of life, often shrouded in mystery. In this sense, the great mural of Huaca Pintada revealed for the first time a monumental support of the sacred iconography of the peoples of the northern coast. It enabled us to glimpse the stories to which the very identity of these people was attached. These images allow us to access the inner narratives of these societies, transcending the biased accounts of Spanish travelers who perceived them through a Christian prism. In this way, these representations serve as a form of traditional ecological knowledge that has been preserved for more than a millennium.

At that time, not only was the field of archaeology still in its infancy, but there were also no laws to protect the cultural heritage of the newly established Peruvian Republic. This lack of regulation allowed widespread looting of ancient sites. In response, a Lambayeque resident named Lorenzo Orrego, captivated by the majesty of a significant discovery, sought to involve local authorities in protecting the site. However, to do so, he needed to stop the looting of the monument. Orrego attempted to prohibit access to the site, but his efforts provoked the anger of the looters. They resented being barred from exploiting a site they had discovered and, in retaliation, destroyed the large painted wall, effectively eliminating any possibility of recovering the monument (Brüning, 1917; Orrego, 1927).

It is important to note that, at the time, looting was not universally regarded as illegal or immoral. For many, it was a casual activity practiced across various social strata. Ambitious individuals might have viewed looting as a source of income, but for others, it was almost a form of recreation (Chirinos, 2018). It was common for families or groups of friends to visit huacas in search of hidden treasures. Wealthier individuals often took pride in photographing themselves at the ruins after clearing the area and would keep material souvenirs as mementos. During Semana Santa (Easter) holidays, families traditionally ventured into fields to uncover relics gifted by Pachamama (Mother Earth). These finds typically consisted of ceramic fragments, embroidered textiles, or small shell beads that had once been part of bracelets or necklaces. This complex and often contradictory relationship with archaeological heritage persists among the inhabitants of Peru's northern coast. Examining these connections – rooted in a hybrid cultural dynamic – is essential for understanding their evolving relationship with history (Soto Roland, 2014) (Fig. 3).

Fortunately, renowned German ethnographer Heinrich Brüning, who explored the valleys of the Lambayeque region from the late 19th century to the early 20th century, made a brief stop at Huaca Pintada (Brüning, 1917). During his visit, he photographed the fresco shortly before its destruction (Figs. 4 and 5). These photographs, later rediscovered by chance in the archives of the Museum of Ethnology in Hamburg, formed the basis for Richard

Fig. 3 A photo dating from 1916 of the looters who discovered the murals of Huaca Pintada (Urteaga, 1917).

Fig. 4 Brüning's photograph of the fresco showing a couple of warriors walking next to a river filled with fish (Schaedel, 1978).

Fig. 5 Another photo from Brüning illustrating a warrior with ornithomorphic traits holding a cup in his hand (Bonavia, 1985).

Fig. 6 Drawing of the left margin of the fresco by Schaedel (1978).

Schaedel's reconstruction of the extraordinary scene (Figs. 6 and 7). Thanks to this effort, we now have a detailed understanding of the fresco's content, which depicts a complex and vibrant narrative.

The fresco portrays a procession of a dozen warriors, illustrated in profile and richly adorned. Each figure carries a mace on one shoulder and an object in the other hand. Some warriors hold cups containing the blood of a sacrificial victim – a ritual typical of Moche ceremonies – while others appear to carry

Fig. 7 Color drawing of the same warrior from Fig. 5 based on Brüning's field notes Schaedel, 1978.

musical instruments or perhaps fruits from their harvest. They are depicted moving toward the center of the scene, where a deity with ornithomorphic features is shown facing forward. Above, a natural setting features rivers teeming with fish and figures engaged in various activities. While it is difficult to determine the definitive meaning of this scene, it seems to represent a sacred order or religious hierarchy. This hierarchy is likely rooted in ancestor worship, emphasizing the intimate relationship between humans and natural forces essential for successful harvests and daily life. Such beliefs persist in some Peruvian communities today, demonstrating their resilience and connection to these ancient traditions (Mariátegui, 1928; Sillar, 2012).

In the century following the creation of this fresco, the religious iconography of the Lambayeque culture prominently featured a tutelary figure resembling a major deity, potentially the image of their legendary founding hero, Ñaimlap (Fig. 8). However, composed scenes like this fresco are rare in Lambayeque art compared to the Moche style. Instead, the Lambayeque people specialized in depicting such imagery on metal artifacts, as seen in the silver bowl of the Priestess of Chornancap or the very elaborate Denver Beaker (Mackey and Pillsbury, 2013; Wester La Torre, 2018).

After the destruction of the fresco, the site was largely abandoned by the scientific community, which assumed there was nothing of value left to study. Compounding the issue, the construction of the Pan-American Highway in the

Fig. 8 Lambayeque golden earring adorning the main deity, Brüning Museum.

1930s divided the site into two sections. It is likely that the remaining vestiges, including the western face of the mound, were destroyed during this process. Over time, news of the site and its discovery faded into obscurity. It was not until more than half a century later that the site regained attention with the publication of Richard Schaedel's work. His findings rekindled interest in this forgotten chapter of history and underscored the significance of the lost fresco.

2.3 Huaca Pintada Today: Getting to Know the Community

In 2014, five years before our first excavations, we had the opportunity to visit the site for the first time. At that point, undertaking a research project felt somewhat distant. However, we deemed it essential to visit the site to assess the current condition of the huaca and to familiarize ourselves with the surrounding community. Much like a church at the heart of a village, the huaca is now central to a hamlet, or *centro poblado*, called La Pintada, which honors its millennia-old heritage. One of the first things that caught our attention was the Pan-American Highway cutting directly through the middle of the hamlet (Fig. 9). Unfortunately, this road poses significant risks as it occasionally claims the lives of individuals attempting to cross. Interestingly, the community attributes these tragic incidents to the huaca, believing that it takes lives when it is hungry.

Stories like these about archaeological sites in Peru are relatively common. While they might seem folkloric at first glance, they reflect a deep and inherently religious connection Peruvians feel toward the ancient vestiges that dot their landscape (León-Barandiarán, 1938; Narváez Vargas, 2014). This bond,

Fig. 9 Aerial view of the Huaca Pintada beneath the trees with the town of Túcume on the background and the Cerro Purgatorio around which 26 pyramids were built.

though it has evolved, traces back to pre-Columbian cultural traditions. For example, in Europe, agency is typically not ascribed to medieval castles. While such structures are considered inhabited by history, they are not viewed as living entities, nor is permission sought from them when visiting. In Peru, by contrast, places like huacas are imbued with spirit and personality. They are perceived as living entities with needs that must be acknowledged and, at times, satisfied or protected. In this way, Peruvians continue to interact with their past in a spiritual and perspectivist manner, a characteristic of the traditional ecological knowledge that defines their worldview (Favaron, 2017; Lau, 2021; Sillar, 2012).

During our first visit, we decided to climb the mound. The ascent proved challenging due to the dense vegetation and numerous trees that have taken root across its surface. This was surprising, as huacas, being constructed from specific building materials, typically do not support significant vegetation growth. They usually stand starkly against their surroundings, uncovered except for layers of sediment. Yet here, the mound was overgrown, presenting an unusual sight that underscored the unique dynamics of this site. The land's distinctive topography was visible, but its structure remained difficult to discern. No architectural features were detectable on the surface. In the more open areas, it was evident that the pyramid had been repeatedly looted, with holes scattered across the site where treasure hunters had searched for valuable artifacts. This suggests that their efforts were fruitful, as this huaca likely contained fine artifacts, stripped of their provenance, now dispersed across private collections worldwide or stored in museum repositories.

Ceramic shards, which could have provided clues about the cultural style and period of occupation, were nearly impossible to find. Instead, the surface was littered with modern debris: items discarded by locals, the remains of dead animals, shells likely originating from nearby restaurants, and what appeared to be offerings left after a recent shamanic ritual. Following this brief exploration, we decided to meet the residents of La Pintada, some of whom we encountered later that afternoon.

The hamlet of La Pintada is home to about a dozen families, though this number has been gradually increasing over the years. Despite its small size, the community boasts three *campestres* restaurants where visitors can enjoy traditional regional dishes, such as *ceviche de caballa*, often served alongside a jar of *chicha de jora* – a fermented corn drink with roots in Andean culture, consumed for thousands of years during sacred festivities (Pease, 2007). The village also has a public school, the Liceo Aguirre La Pintada, founded in 1935 by the father of its current director, Professor Cobeñas Inoñán, who was born just five years after the school's establishment.

One of the school's neighbors, Mr. Félix Llauce, greeted us at his doorstep and recommended we speak with Professor Cobeñas if we wanted to learn more about the site. Though our conversation with Mr. Llauce was brief, we could sense the depth of connection he felt to this place. It was clear that the presence of the huaca had shaped many stories within his family, infusing the community with a unique sense of identity and history.

Professor Cobeñas Inoñán

Don Vidal Cobeñas is one of the elders of La Pintada, deeply familiar with the village's recent history and always eager to share stories with visitors. He is gracious man with a stern gaze and an impeccable sense of uprightness that he instills in his students, but who also possesses a warmth and generosity that made us feel immediately welcome in his office. After studying philosophy and theology in Lima, he returned to La Pintada, proud of his native land, which had also nurtured one of Peru's greatest mathematicians, Federico Villarreal. In Don Vidal, we encountered a striking blend of scientific rigor inspired by the rationalist traditions of the Enlightenment, a profound Christian faith, and a deep immersion in the cultural heritage of his Indigenous roots (Fig. 10).

Before we sat down, Don Vidal enthusiastically showed us a photograph of himself with Richard Schaedel, taken during Schaedel's visit to La Pintada in the

Fig. 10 Professor Vidal Cobeñas in his office.

1980s. Schaedel, likely curious to see the site he had written about, had made a trip to the village following his publication. Don Vidal also recounted anecdotes about Thor Heyerdahl, the adventurer behind the famed Kon-Tiki expedition of the late 1940s. Heyerdahl's journey had demonstrated that ancient peoples might have reached Polynesia from Peru on simple rafts carried by ocean currents (Heyerdahl, 1950). Thor had even purchased a house in the region, drawn by the pyramids of Túcume, and thought he detected a connection between the ornithomorphic deities depicted in this part of Peru and those of the Pacific Islands.

The professor spoke about Huaca Pintada with a palpable sense of reverence, describing its aura and its once-prized treasure – the magnificent mural painting, which he sadly never saw himself. We took the opportunity to ask him about the fresco and whether his father had shared any anecdotes about looters. However, he offered little new information beyond what Schaedel had already documented nearly 40 years ago. Nonetheless, he provided valuable insights about the style of ceramics found at the site, which became the starting point for our investigation.

Professor Cobeñas was perhaps one of the people most interested in learning about the history of the huaca, a history that lay buried, and he understood that an archaeological investigation was necessary to reconnect the past with the present.

Fig. 11 The school Liceo Aguirre La Pintada of Túcume.

Given his position as an educator, he proved to be an indispensable agent not only in transmitting new knowledge to his students but also in rescuing a history and a cultural heritage that belongs to them and that would contribute to strengthening their identity. In addition to the family nucleus, the community school is an important space for sociocultural reproduction in which this traditional ecological knowledge is disseminated. In this capacity, Don Vidal acts as a mediator, bridging the paradigms of Western education and Indigenous knowledge. He integrates these two perspectives into a modern curriculum, ensuring that the heritage of the huaca remains relevant. Furthermore, as a respected voice in the community, he serves as a source of guidance and consultation, actively transmitting new knowledge and fostering an appreciation of their cultural inheritance among the people of La Pintada (Figs. 11 and 12).

The Granados Family

Our brief visit to the site in 2014 confirmed our intuition that understanding the community around La Pintada would be essential before initiating an excavation project. A few years later, in 2018, we founded the Huaca Pintada Archaeological Investigation Project (PIAHP) to organize the excavation of

Fig. 12 A visit from the students of Professor Vidal at the site while we were digging.

the site, supported by a grant from the Swiss National Science Foundation (SNF). The first step was securing the collaboration of archaeologist Bernarda Delgado Elías, the director of the Túcume Museum, which oversees archaeological interventions in the La Leche Valley region.

The major state museums in this area are not only cultural hubs for preserving ancient and contemporary traditions; they also serve as research centers that conduct large-scale excavations and actively disseminate new knowledge to the public. Delgado offered her support but explained that the Túcume Museum had previously attempted to include Huaca Pintada in their research project. Unfortunately, they were forced to abandon the effort due to a disagreement with a community member. She noted that the main pyramid is legally situated on private land owned by the Granados family. The patriarch, Don Augusto, is particularly cautious about state intervention, fearing the risk of expropriation.

Although the site is officially recognized as Peruvian national heritage, any intervention – including by the Granados family – requires authorization from the Ministry of Culture. However, the lack of precise demarcation of the archaeological zone complicates matters. Without clear boundaries, it is impossible to definitively determine where the protected heritage zone ends and private land begins. Such ambiguities are not uncommon in Peru, where heritage protection laws were implemented relatively late (Dube, 2014; Uribe-Chinen, 2024). As a result, many sites – particularly smaller ones without significant discoveries to prompt their formal recognition – remain unregulated.

This situation is further complicated by historically contentious relationships between the state and local communities, particularly concerning landownership and usage rights. Claims of expropriation, whether for archaeological preservation or natural resource exploitation, persist to this day (Anaya, 2014;

Morales, 2024). Adding to the tension are criminal groups that exert violent pressure to seize land, often for developing new neighborhoods and profiting from renting out spaces to disadvantaged individuals. These overlapping challenges have fostered a climate of mistrust among the various stakeholders, each convinced of the legitimacy of their claims (Kania, 2019).

According to Schaedel's 1978 paper, the land was owned by a certain Marcelo Granados as early as 1916. Our research confirms that Don Augusto is Marcelo's grandson, and the Granados family has likely lived on this land since the mid 19th century or even earlier. For the Granados family, the huaca is not only a national monument but also a deeply personal inheritance woven into their family identity over generations. Don Augusto often refers to the huaca as a structure built by his own ancestors in ancient times, reinforcing the sense of personal and familial ownership over the site.

Augusto Granados is a man of strong character in his 70s, a trait that has only deepened since the loss of his wife to cancer. His home is tucked away in a remote corner east of the huaca, accessible only by navigating a bramble-filled path. Visitors are first met by his barking dogs, which loudly announce anyone daring to approach his front door. We had no idea at the time that this ritual of cautious approach would become a recurring challenge throughout our project. Don Augusto, for a period, wanted nothing to do with us. A lifelong farmer, he worked the land surrounding the huaca to support his family. From his marriage, he had three sons who still live nearby and a daughter who moved to Argentina, where she married. His youngest son, Ronald, recently turned 40 and shared with us his hopes for a fresh start, aspiring to live up to his responsibilities as a father and husband. Ronald ultimately became a valuable ally, helping us gain access to the site.

Our first meeting with Don Augusto went smoothly. When he emerged from his house, we briefly introduced ourselves. He extended a rough hand, hardened by decades of farmwork, and invited us to sit on three chairs he pulled out. Don Augusto spoke freely, sharing family stories, describing the ceramics his grandfather once owned, and recounting the fear the huaca inspired in those who dared to visit it late at night. His initial openness left us confident about the feasibility of our project. However, things took an unexpected turn a few months later when he informed us of his opposition to the excavation (Fig. 13).

This marked the beginning of a long and challenging negotiation process we had not anticipated during our first visit. When we returned to La Pintada the following year to commence our excavation campaign, it was clear that Don Augusto's attitude had shifted. Unbeknownst to us, he had received a formal notice from the Ministry of Culture about the project, leading him to believe we were working on behalf of the Peruvian state.

Fig. 13 Don Augusto Granados sitting in front of his house.

Given his mistrust of state authorities, often perceived as neglectful in such matters, he became wary of our intentions. Suddenly, the idea of excavating the site had transformed into a significant obstacle.

Seeking advice from archaeologist colleagues and friends, we were often told to involve the police, as we had the necessary authorization from the Ministry of Culture to proceed. However, we firmly rejected this approach. Imposing ourselves in such a manner was unthinkable, especially as outsiders to the region. We believed it was crucial to establish a foundation of trust for the project. Open conflict with a family living right next to the site posed enormous risks: Someone could sabotage the excavation units at night, destroy unearthed structures, or even threaten our team. None of this aligned with the principles of archaeological research, which seeks to build connections rather than sever them.

Recognizing the need for a different approach, we focused on understanding the customs and perspectives of the local community to navigate the situation effectively. After all, local problems demand local solutions. Bridging these divides required patience and sensitivity, as the very essence of studying the past is to foster links – not destroy them.

Don José Jesús, the Shaman

As it became clear that reconciliation with the Granados family would require time, an urgent decision was necessary to devise an alternative plan as the team was already prepared to begin work. To avoid escalating tensions and losing the field campaign entirely, we decided to focus our initial excavations on the western sector of the site, located on the other side of the road. This area was not part of Don Augusto's land, making it a more feasible starting point.

During the first campaign in 2019, we stayed with several team members at the Túcume Museum. Anthropologist Ana Mariella Bacigalupo, a professor at the University of Buffalo, was also staying there at the time to conduct her fieldwork on shamanism along Peru's northern coast. We had the chance to exchange insights on several occasions, and when we described the challenges surrounding the Huaca Pintada excavations, she mentioned meeting a shaman who worked with the spirit of the huaca. She suggested we speak with him. Although the idea initially seemed unconventional, it quickly became clear that engaging with this perspective could be essential to navigating the situation.

A few days later, a large gathering of more than 40 shamans took place at the Túcume archaeological site, presenting the perfect opportunity to meet Don José Jesús Sandoval Morales, the shaman Bacigalupo had mentioned. That evening, the anthropologist introduced us to several shamans she knew through her research. The gathering's atmosphere was electrifying, with a palpable energy in the air. The shamans, dressed in their characteristic ponchos and hats, were surrounded by people seeking their counsel. Services ranged from simple consultations to *limpiezas* (spiritual purifications) and more elaborate rituals, some involving the consumption of San Pedro – a cactus containing mescaline, known for its psychedelic properties (Bohn et al., 2022). The scale and intensity of the event underscored the significant role shamanism plays in the cultural fabric of Peru's northern coast (Sharon, 1978).

For an outside observer, the question is not whether one believes in shamanism but rather understanding its pivotal role in this society, where shamans are recognized as essential figures. Watching the individuals flocking to them, it became apparent that their function parallels that of traditional healers. Many of the issues brought to them were health-related, but unlike Western doctors, shamans rely on knowledge imparted by spiritual beings – *dueños espirituales* (spiritual owners) – during transcendental visions that connect them to super-sensory worlds (Favaron, 2017). But beyond healing, shamans are also trusted mediators in societal conflicts, acting as intermediaries between disputing parties (Bacigalupo, 2019, personal communication).

Fig. 14 A congregation of shamans in the site of Túcume. Photo was taken by Ana Mariella Bacigalupo.

In our context, this role of mediation was crucial. To ease the tensions surrounding the excavation, we needed a voice to represent our position in the traditional terms understood and respected by the community. Engaging with Don José Jesús Sandoval Morales and the shamanic framework offered a culturally rooted approach to address the challenges we faced, ensuring our efforts aligned with the local perspective (Fig. 14).

After some time, we finally encountered Don José Jesús along a path, seated behind his shamanic altar. His *mesa curandera* was arranged with a variety of objects, known as *artes*, each with specific ritual significance. These included seashells, wooden effigies shaped like snakes or human faces, Christian crosses and saints' relics, as well as swords, stones, pre-Columbian ceramics (sometimes modern replicas), and other relics. Each item served a distinct function during the ritual, carefully positioned on the altar to invoke the spirit it embodied. American anthropologist Donald Joralemon (1985, p. 5) described the mesa as "a concrete representation of hallucinatory imagery presented through symbols charged with cultural significance," functioning as "a kind of visionary map that helps the shaman maintain control over his drug experience."

That evening, Don José Jesús appeared agitated, holding a glass of *yonque* (sugar cane liquor) while the bottle sat at his feet. As we began explaining the purpose of

Fig. 15 Don José Jesús preparing a ritual next to his *mesa curandera*.

our visit, he seemed reluctant to engage. Fortunately, Mariella was able to persuade him to meet with us at his home the following morning to organize a ritual. The next day, at 10:00 a.m., we visited him in the *caserío* San Bernardino. This time, he was friendly and he and his family welcomed us warmly. He decided to perform a ritual that evening, with the assistance of another *curandero* who had traveled from the Andes for the Túcume congregation. The purpose of the ritual was to invoke the spirit of Huaca Pintada to accept our presence, which in turn, it was believed, would influence Don Augusto Granados to accept us as well (Fig. 15).

That evening, we returned with Mariella Bacigalupo to participate in the ritual. It began around 8:00 p.m. and lasted nearly eight hours. The experience was at times hazy, as we often felt drowsy during the long proceedings. We sat in a small outdoor space, enveloped by the pitch-black night. Before the ritual commenced, we anointed ourselves with floral perfumes and herbs to purify body and soul. Don José Jesús and Don Pedro, the other shaman, began singing their *tarjo*s – magical songs intended to guide us through the ritual – accompanied by the rhythmic sound of a rattle called a *chungana*. The ceremony was occasionally interrupted by a neighbor seeking treatment for his feverish son or by hens and turkeys wandering through the yard.

Shamanism is an ancient spiritual practice that dates back to the Formative Period in the Andes (circa 2000–200 BC), deeply rooted in Indigenous cosmologies and healing traditions (Rick, 2015; Small, 2001; Viveiros de Castro, 2007). However, it was striking to see how deeply syncretic or hybrid the nature of shamanic practices is on Peru's northern coast. The shamans' songs invoked specific spirits but always began with references to the Blessed Virgin Mary, Jesus, and, on several occasions, Saint Cyprian of Carthage.[2] Over time, it has evolved by incorporating new elements, such as the veneration of Catholic saints, yet certain fundamental aspects persist. The connection with nature, the use of medicinal plants, and the role of the shaman as an intermediary between the human and spiritual realms remain central to these practices. While historical and cultural transformations have shaped shamanic rituals, the continuity of core beliefs – such as the importance of spiritual balance and ancestral wisdom – demonstrates how tradition adapts without losing its essence. This dynamic interplay between change and permanence highlights the resilience of shamanism as a living tradition, maintaining its relevance in contemporary Peruvian society.

Furthermore, this cultural blend is emblematic of modern Peru, where Indigenous traditions have been transformed and adapted through European influences (Favaron, 2017; Sharon, 1978). Whether in Lima's affluent neighborhoods or in Peru's most remote regions, the mark of Indigenous culture, reshaped by colonial encounters, remains indelible. Despite the brutal repressions of the colonial era, Indigenous traditions did not disappear but instead evolved within the imposed framework, demonstrating remarkable resilience over the centuries.

This syncretism illustrates the inefficacy of arguing for a supposed "purity" of pre-Columbian culture in contemporary communities. Modern Peruvian culture is part of a vast and dynamic historical continuum. Just as archaeological artifacts cannot be frozen in time as static museum exhibits, cultures and traditions adapt, evolve, and trace their own trajectories. Similarly, the traditional knowledge Indigenous communities have accumulated over recent centuries has been enriched by this cultural fusion, embodying the resilience and adaptability that define their identity (Doughty, 2014; Favaron, 2017; Kania, 2019; Sillar, 2012).

---

[2] In popular culture, Saint Cyprian of Carthage is revered for undoing witchcraft and works of black magic (Leitão, 2014).

By the end of the ritual, we were exhausted, but with only a few hours of rest, we had to return to work with the entire team. The decision to consult the shaman had not been unanimous, and we sincerely hoped for favorable results to avoid further discouragement. Patience was key as the ritual itself was just one step in a longer process. Don José Jesús took it upon himself to ensure its effectiveness. Over the following days, he visited Don Augusto, engaging him in conversation over a few glasses of chicha. During these visits, he casually mentioned meeting young archaeologists, including one who had traveled from Switzerland to study Huaca Pintada. Initially wary, Don Augusto eventually admitted that he did not harbor ill will toward us but was concerned that the Ministry of Culture might overlook his family's long-standing efforts to preserve the site.

The first field season ended in the hope that the relationship could be restored when coming back. During the Covid-19 pandemic, we made a concerted effort to stay in touch with both our team and the community of La Pintada. Peru was one of the countries hardest hit by the pandemic, and during this time, Don José Jesús lost his father. Recognizing their need, we contributed to the funeral costs to express our support, even though we could not be there in person. The gesture was deeply appreciated, and Don José Jesús mentioned it to Don Augusto, which helped renew contact. Don Augusto, a man who values traditional ties and family bonds – values he feels are increasingly fragile – was moved by the act.

The Chapoñán Family

At the foot of Huaca Pintada is the La Huaca restaurant, a traditional *picantería* run by the Chapoñán family for more than 20 years. During our first visit to the site, we met Maricela, one of the four daughters of Doña Clotilde Chapoñán and head chef since the tragic loss of her only brother, Justo Iván, in a road accident a few years earlier. Justo Iván had shown great promise, representing northern Peruvian gastronomy at major national fairs from a young age. Despite this tragedy, Maricela remained warm and collaborative, eager to support our project. During our conversations, she shared stories about the huaca and revealed that Don Augusto Granados was her uncle by marriage.

When we returned for the second field season in September 2021, we planned to meet Don Augusto again to secure permission to access the site. Unfortunately, his health had deteriorated, and we were unable to speak with him directly. With time running out, we realized we could no longer afford to excavate anywhere other than the east sector, where the main pyramid is located. We turned to the Chapoñán family and asked for their permission to place excavation units in the outdoor courtyard of their restaurant.

Fig. 16 The Chapoñán family in their restaurant. Milagros is sitting in the center next to her kids and her uncle. Doña Clotilde stands in the back.

The courtyard of La Huaca is located less than 10 meters from the north side of Huaca Pintada, making it a promising area for uncovering evidence of past occupation near the archaeological monument. Maricela's sister Milagros had since taken over the kitchen, and in consultation with their mother, they gladly granted us permission. Milagros, with her characteristic cheerfulness, remarked that she hoped the excavation would at least bring more customers to the restaurant (Fig. 16).

Over the course of the project, we developed a deep friendship with the Chapoñán family, built on genuine trust and mutual respect. They were eager to see what we might uncover on their land and offered invaluable logistical support throughout our work. Their restaurant became the perfect spot for our team's lunch breaks, where they served us excellent traditional meals every day. Additionally, they provided us with a secure room to store our excavation tools, sparing us the burden of carrying them back and forth daily. This room also became our workspace for cleaning and conserving artifacts, such as ceramic fragments, which we processed alongside the excavations. The family's generosity extended to our celebrations as well – team members' birthdays that fell on workdays were marked with joyous gatherings organized with the active participation of the Chapoñáns (Fig. 17).

Fig. 17 Maricela Chapoñán in her kitchen holding a jar of chicha.

The Inoñán Tantarico Family

In the project's first year, we focused on excavating the west sector of the site. Before beginning, we made it a priority to meet the landowners to avoid potential conflicts similar to those with the Granados family. This part of Huaca Pintada is surrounded by extensive agricultural fields and a few modern dwellings, which have somewhat altered its appearance. The area features an artificial elevation, heavily eroded by numerous looting pits, making it difficult to discern any clear architectural patterns with the naked eye. Since the main pyramid is not located in this sector, negotiations with the community were more straightforward. During this time, Maricela Chapoñán mentioned another restaurant on this side of the road.

The Potrero restaurant was run by the Inoñán Tantarico family, who also owned some plots of land within the archaeological zone. We were introduced to Giovanna, the eldest daughter, who managed the kitchen while her sister handled table service and her children played nearby. Her parents were always present, lending a hand with daily tasks. Giovanna's mother, dressed daily in traditional Lambayeque clothing, brewed the famous chicha every week in large

Fig. 18 Giovanna Inoñán and her mother in their restaurant, El Potrero.

pots, following the same methods as her ancestors. Over a carafe of chicha, we got to know Giovanna, who graciously showed us areas where we could excavate without issue. This marked the point where the project finally got underway, despite a short delay and a temporary adjustment to our objectives (Fig. 18).

In this region, chicha is deeply cherished. This ancient beverage is considered sacred by local communities and remains especially popular in rural areas and the Potrero has a reputation for producing some of the best chicha in Lambayeque. As project directors, we decided to incorporate this tradition into our daily routine: at 4:00 p.m., an hour before wrapping up for the day, we would visit the Potrero to purchase two large bottles of chicha, which we shared with the team on the huaca. Working all day under the scorching desert sun of Peru's northern coast was taxing, and this simple refreshment provided a much-needed break. However, the gesture was also symbolic. Members of the community who worked in the project appreciated the ritual, often inviting us to

Fig. 19 Sharing the chicha with our team during the visit of archaeologist Carlos Elera.

toast with the huaca. As a mark of gratitude, we poured the last drops of our glasses onto the earth, symbolizing our respect for the site and its permission to study it. These moments of reciprocity strengthened our bonds with the community, fostering friendships that extended beyond the academic goals of the project. More than just a routine gesture, this practice became a cornerstone of our approach, aligning with local customs to foster trust and mutual respect. By embedding this methodology into our work, we attempted to demonstrate a commitment to Indigenous relationality, ensuring that our collaboration was guided by cultural sensitivity and shared values (Smith, 1999). (Fig. 19)

Excavation Technicians

A key priority when starting the project was to involve as many community members as possible. No one knew the site better than they did, and their genuine interest in our work was evident during every conversation about the excavation. Through discussions with local families, we learned about individuals who had prior experience working on archaeological digs and were eager to collaborate with us. As a result, in addition to Nayo Solano and Don Damian Quiroz – both of whom had been long-time collaborators with us at the San José de Moro site in the Jequetepeque Valley – we enlisted three additional technicians from the region: Lucho Granados (a cousin of Don Augusto Granados), Jacinto Sandoval, and Don Teo Sandoval. During the second and third excavation campaigns, the team expanded to include Víctor Bravo, Miguel Santamaría, Ronald Cisneros, and Meche Suclupe.

These individuals rank among the most skilled diggers we've ever worked with. Some of the older team members had participated in illicit excavations before transitioning their expertise to scientific and legitimate archaeological projects. Their deep experience and unique knowledge of the land allow them to detect even the subtlest changes in soil composition, often anticipating discoveries before they fully emerge. Their precision and patience in excavation are remarkable, ensuring that the individuals they unearth are revealed in near-perfect condition.

In addition to local technicians, we chose to work exclusively with students from Pedro Ruiz Gallo University in Lambayeque. Luigui Oliva, whose keen interest in the transitional period between the Moche and Lambayeque cultures had inspired his involvement from the project's inception, became an invaluable team member. He was later joined by seven other students, several of whom are now writing their bachelor's theses on specific aspects of Huaca Pintada.

The success of this project is inseparable from the contributions of this dedicated team. Their skills, passion, and unwavering support were instrumental in achieving the convincing results we obtained. Without their collaboration, it is certain that the project would not have reached the level of success it enjoys today, and we owe them immense gratitude for their indispensable role (Figs. 20 and 21).

The Calvay Inoñán Family

When organizing the first excavation campaign in the west sector, we prioritized meeting with families living near the archaeological area. Our goal was to identify a space to store our tools and to explore the possibility of arranging daily lunches under conditions that worked for everyone. This led us to meet Doña Paula Calvay Inoñán, who lived with her family in a house behind the archaeological mound. During that first campaign, before we established an arrangement with the Chapoñán family in later seasons, Doña Paula prepared delicious family recipes for us every day. After lunch, she generously let us rest in her courtyard, where hammocks and benches nestled among her chickens and turkeys provided a peaceful reprieve before the afternoon's work.

A humorous anecdote: Every morning throughout the month-long excavations, one of her hens laid an egg in the back seat of our moto-taxi. Over time, as our team grew larger, we maintained our relationship with Doña Paula. Some

Fig. 20 Nayo patiently exhuming an individual from the ground.

team members continued to have lunch at her house while others dined at La Huaca, ensuring that multiple families benefitted from our presence in the community (Fig. 22).

As our work progressed, the excavation began to draw the attention of passersby, many of whom came to see what we had discovered. This curiosity provided an excellent opportunity to engage with the community and explain the purpose of our work and the importance of preserving the archaeological monument. We discovered that many visitors did not initially understand the difference between the work of archaeologists and that of looters and were surprised to learn that we did not keep the artifacts for ourselves. These interactions became a daily occurrence and allowed us to meet a significant portion of the community as word of our project spread (Fig. 23).

Conflict Resolution

Before beginning any excavation project in Peru, it is customary to perform a *pago a la Pachamama*, an offering to Mother Earth or directly to the huaca. This ceremony seeks the favor of the huaca to be studied, with the hope of

Fig. 21 Don Damian and Nayo teaching the student how to recognize the adobe bricks from the western façade of the huaca.

Fig. 22 Our team during the first excavations from 2019 with Doña Calvay.

Fig. 23 Doña Calvay's family visiting during the excavations.

achieving positive outcomes and smooth progress during the work. The ritual gathers participants in a circle around one or more pre-dug holes, into which they offer items such as corn, sweets – in our case, small Swiss chocolates – and a toast of *yonque* (local liquor), first drinking part of the glass and then pouring the rest into the hole. It is a deeply shared moment of connection, opening participants to ancestral spirituality. This gathering also fosters team cohesion, cultivating mutual respect not only among team members but also toward the place of study itself, creating a bond between humans and the nonhuman world (Alderman, 2021).

We invited Don José Jesús to guide the ritual during our second campaign, recognizing that he was uniquely suited for the role. Involving him in this way helped integrate him into the project, ensuring he shared our commitment to its success (Fig. 24). At the end of the ceremony, Don José confided that the signals he perceived from the huaca were positive and that we would achieve our goals. While relieved by his words, we remained cautious as the excavation units near the restaurant had yet to yield significant results. There was little material evidence of occupation and no trace of the murals. However, the time spent on-site allowed us to reconnect with the Granados family, who lived nearby.

This renewed connection began when Lucho, one of our excavation collaborators, ran into his uncle, Don Augusto, at the local market. He used the

Fig. 24 Don José Jesús performing during the *pago a la huaca*.

opportunity to discuss the value of studying the pyramid and how discovering traces of the mural could benefit the entire community. During that time, we invited Ronald Granados to visit the excavation site to observe our working methods and see our good intentions firsthand. Initially, Ronald was somewhat distant, feeling that our activities inconvenienced his father. Over time, however, trust began to grow. Unlike his father, Ronald recognized the potential of having a research project on their land. He recognized that without open collaboration between his family and our archaeological project, none of us would be able to benefit from the site. He therefore expressed his interest in cooperating, on the condition of his father's approval.

Like other community members, Ronald warned us about the risks of excavating Huaca Pintada, which many believed was inhabited by an evil spirit. This belief, he explained, stemmed from accidents that had occurred near the site. We acknowledged his concerns but felt that this perspective may be reductive – not in its spiritual essence, but in its omission to recognize that the huaca, like any living being, could embody both positive and negative qualities. To address this warning, we proposed that such a perception of the huaca might stem from our own lack of knowledge. It was therefore crucial to shift this viewpoint and make a genuine effort to get to know *her*. Our interest in studying the huaca was rooted in discovering who she was and understanding the messages she held. By fostering this connection, we believe, learning about others ultimately deepens our self-respect, which forms the foundation for mutual care.

The next weekend, Ronald invited us to meet at the El Potrero restaurant. To our surprise and relief, he shared that his father was now open to allowing us to work on Huaca Pintada. Don Augusto Granados requested that local archaeologists and technicians also be involved in investigating the huaca, as he feared losing the ancestral knowledge that it embodied. Determined to reach an agreement that benefited all parties, we proposed hiring Ronald as a guardian of the site during the excavations. This solution offered immediate proof of goodwill while compensating the family for granting access to their land. Additionally, we offered to assist Don Augusto in acquiring medication he needed and, because he was also deeply frustrated by the state's failure to recognize his ancestral lands, we propose to act as intermediaries with the Ministry of Culture to delineate the intangible archaeological zone around Huaca Pintada. The primary source of the conflict had been the Ministry of Culture's lack of consultation with Don Augusto, leaving him aggrieved by the initial proposal, which designated part of his farmland as protected heritage. Our proposal sought a balanced delimitation that respected both archaeological priorities and the family's needs while making clear that the final decision rested with the Ministry of Culture. These steps were fundamentals, as we consider that research is not merely an academic pursuit but also an ethical and moral responsibility. The success of a project like this one stemmed from its commitment to honoring and following the local needs and traditions.

Following this meeting, we were thrilled to announce to our team that we had finally secured permission to study the monument. Those closest to the process, who had followed the challenges from the start, were as eager as we were to begin work. After years of effort, we were relieved and excited to finally search for the remnants of the lost fresco.

2.4 Lessons for Future Archaeological Research

The experience of gaining access to Huaca Pintada site highlights the crucial importance of establishing strong communication and cooperation with the surrounding local communities. We have seen that it is necessary from the beginning to seek to know the various key members of the community who live around the site and to learn its history. Only by committing in this way will we be able to establish relationships of trust that can develop throughout the execution of the work and lead to better learning about local customs and, ultimately, access to traditional ecological knowledge (see, for example, Huambachano and Cooper, 2020).

Archaeological research projects must contribute as much as they can to the active life of the community and its local economy by providing employment opportunities linked to the execution of the work – excavation technicians, meal organizations, site guardians, etcetera – but also to present the results of their research by welcoming visitors to the site or by presenting the results directly to the local school. By feeling involved in the process, the community will necessarily be more interested in the project and will more easily come to help resolve unexpected situations to which they will be able to respond better than us (Cusicanqui Marsano, 2023).

Also, it is essential to respect local beliefs and practices while taking into account the needs of the community. So it is imperative to pay attention to them in an attempt to understand the values held by these societies to maintain mutual respect (Huambachano and Cooper, 2020; Kania, 2019). This also helps avoid conflicts. As we have seen in the case of the Granados family, the solution came through different actors respecting the cultural codes of the community, but also through learning more about Don Augusto's concern about the recognition of his land. In sum, the experience at Huaca Pintada underscores the importance of the inclusion of local communities and interdisciplinary cooperation to carry out fruitful and socially responsible archaeological research.

3 Archaeology, Conservation, and Preservation of Huaca Pintada

Our decision to excavate Huaca Pintada stemmed from the hypothesis that the site's initial occupation could date back to the Transitional Period on the northern coast of Peru (Ghavami, 2021; Rucabado and Castillo, 2003). The fresco's pictorial style appears to blend elements of traditional Moche canons with emerging forms characteristic of Lambayeque art (Schaedel, 1978). Thus the excavation aimed to uncover data that could enhance our understanding of the complex social dynamics during this period of significant change in the La Leche-Motupe Valley. A key objective in our investigation was to locate traces of the murals in situ, which could enable us to contextualize the painted wall and infer its function.

Huaca Pintada is a pyramidal mound located on the left bank of the La Leche River, approximately 1 kilometer north of the modern town of Túcume in the Lambayeque department. Historically associated with the town of Illimo, shifting political boundaries have since placed it within the Túcume district. The construction of the Pan-American Highway in 1930 significantly impacted the site, dividing it into two sections. The western sector is surrounded by extensive cultivated fields and modern houses, which have caused considerable damage to the structures that once existed there. The surface of this sector bears numerous looting pits from various periods. In contrast, the eastern sector features the main pyramidal mound and has suffered the most damage from human activities. The monument's current dimensions are approximately 100 by 75 by 8 meters. On its western side, an adobe façade, likely exposed during the road's construction, remains visible beneath dense vegetation (Fig. 25).

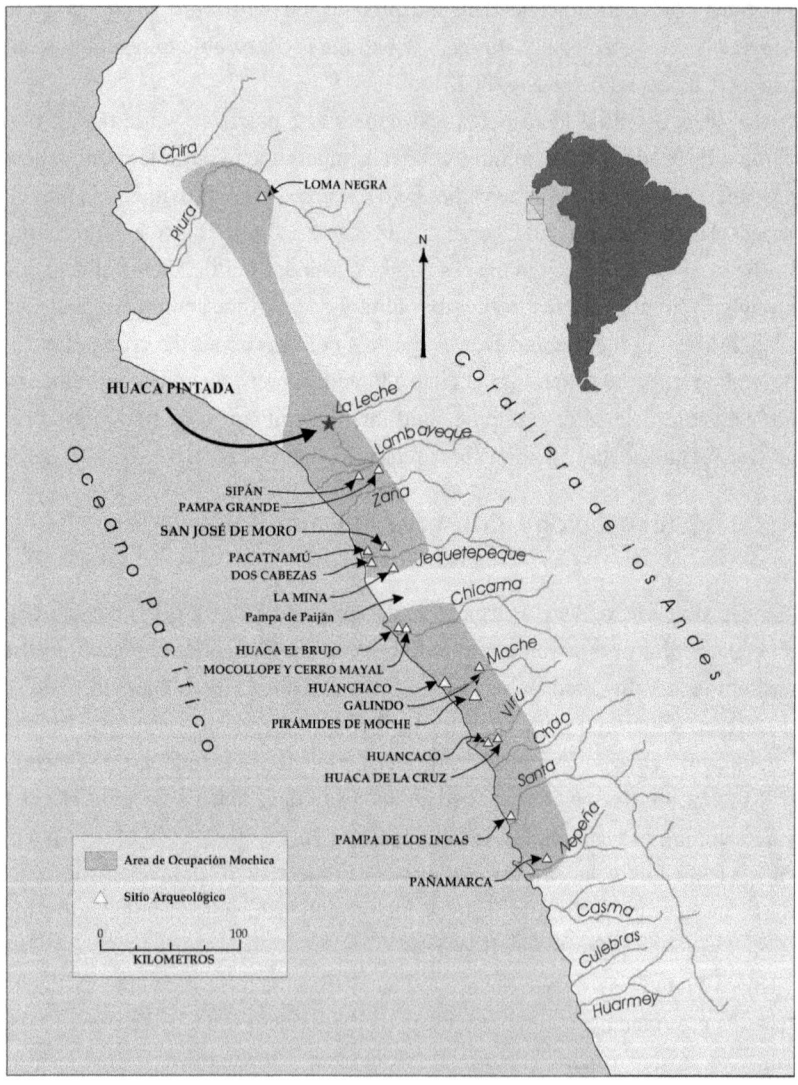

Fig. 25 Map of the northern coast of Perú and location of the Huaca Pintada archaeological site (PASJM archives).

Huaca Pintada occupies a unique position within the La Leche-Motupe Valley, situated midway between several key settlements and religious centers of the Lambayeque culture across its various periods. Nearby, the Illimo cemetery housed the burial of an elite warrior alongside numerous other significant funerary contexts from a similar era (Hepfer, 2017; Martínez Fiestas, 2014). Further to the northeast, approximately 7 kilometers away, the illustrious Sicán lords established their capital in the Pómac forest. This site featured impressive mausoleums and a massive production of prestigious goods, symbolizing the height of their dynasty during the Middle Period (Shimada, 1995). To the southwest, toward the sea, Huaca Pintada connects with the La Pava site, known for its production centers (Fernández Manayalle, 2016). Finally, 1 kilometer to the southeast, the monumental pyramids of Túcume played a pivotal role in later periods up to the Spanish arrival (Heyerdahl, Sandweiss, and Narváez Vargas, 1995). Understanding Huaca Pintada's occupation requires considering its dynamic interactions and negotiations with these and other significant sites in the valley's history.

During two field seasons, we conducted direct interventions on the main pyramid, studying three specific sectors: (1) the west façade of the temple, (2) the northern flank, and (3) the central section at the top of the huaca.

The west façade, partially damaged by the construction of the Pan-American Highway, was profiled to study the construction sequence of the main structure. This approach quickly revealed the architectural techniques employed and the type of adobe bricks used. The evidence pointed to two distinct phases: an initial phase involving the preparation and construction of the structure, followed by a phase marked by a ritual of abandonment. This ritual involved covering the pyramid with clean sand, effectively burying the architecture. Such practices were common on Peru's northern coast, though their purpose remains a topic of debate (Uceda, 2010). One interpretation is that this burial mirrored funerary traditions, suggesting the huaca itself was treated as a living entity with its own spirit (Muro Ynoñán, 2023).

No evidence of prior occupation was found at the site, as indicated by a sterile layer immediately beneath the pyramid. Additionally, the absence of formal architectural remains in the northern sector suggests that Huaca Pintada had a relatively short period of use, likely less than 100 years.

Due to poor surface conditions and the numerous *algarrobo* trees growing on the site, a clear visualization of the architecture was initially impossible. Preliminary observations suggested that the huaca was oriented to the east. Excavations on the northern flank revealed that the pyramid was enclosed by a large perimeter wall delineating interior and exterior spaces. This provided initial insights into the architectural pattern, which included a main platform

Fig. 26 The retaining walls forming the "chamber and fill" technique from Unit 2.

elevated through a series of retaining walls (Fig. 26). These walls formed enclosed compartments used in the "chamber and fill" construction technique. This method involved filling the compartments with sand, organic material, or ceramic debris to efficiently raise the structure's height (Shimada, 1995).

The most intriguing section was the central area at the top of the huaca, where we uncovered a large plaza connected to the main platform by a central ramp. This area revealed at least one phase of remodeling during which spaces were slightly restructured, and some original walls were covered with newly painted plaster. These findings highlighted the huaca's complex construction process. Our primary focus concentrated on this area, as it was the most likely location for traces of the fresco. Lorenzo Orrego and Heinrich Brüning, the only individuals to have seen the fresco firsthand, published descriptions of the paintings but provided no precise information about its location. The most significant clue was that they were painted on the inner faces of the outer walls of the pyramid, described as a "construction composed of several

Fig. 27 Excavations of the area on top the huaca under the watchful eyes of Don Augusto and Ronald Granados.

compartments that communicated with each other, enclosed by walls forming a quadrilateral" (Bennett, 1939, p. 117). Orrego estimated the superficial extent to be around 650 square meters, excluding "collapsed parts." Since the huaca is six times larger, it is likely he was referring to the top of the monument, assuming the rest of the platform comprised the collapsed areas (Fig. 27).

Based on this reasoning, we opened an excavation unit in 2021 and documented hundreds of wall fragments across a full section of the floor. Most fragments were painted red, with a few displaying designs. While these traces suggested we had found remnants of murals, the style indicated they belonged to a different fresco, not the one we sought. Field evidence suggests this wall was likely destroyed during pre-Hispanic times rather than in the past century by looters. Despite this, we felt we were on the right track. When we returned in 2022, Don Granados granted us access to the huaca from the outset, allowing us to focus our efforts on the sector near the main plaza and the painted fragments (Fig. 28).

After weeks of excavation, a breakthrough came when we consulted a 1917 magazine and discovered previously unknown photographs of the Huaca Pintada murals (Urteaga, 1917, p. 450). Although the images were of poor quality, two details caught our attention. First, the face of the wall appeared to

Fig. 28 Fragments of painted wall that may have been destroyed during pre-Hispanic times.

Fig. 29 Photos of the fresco showing a bit of shadow covering the paintings (Urteaga, 1917).

incline backward. Second, shadows partially obscured the paintings. These observations led us to deduce that the wall's orientation likely followed a north–south axis rather than an east–west one. In an east–west orientation, sunlight would illuminate the wall's inner face throughout the day due to the sun's trajectory. However, with a north–south orientation, illumination would vary depending on the time of day, consistent with the shadowing observed in the photographs (Fig. 29).

The excavations revealed that the site's walls had precise orientations. In Unit 6, we identified a sturdy wall that not only displayed traces of red coloring but

Fig. 30 The discovery of the murals while detecting traces of black and red paintings from the headdress of a warrior.

also had a face inclined backward. However, it was not the mural we had hoped to find. Adapting our strategy, we expanded the excavation on both sides of the unit to locate the wall's corners, allowing us to project two new trenches toward the midsection of the huaca in the hope of uncovering the murals in one of them.

Our efforts paid off when, after lightly scraping the soil in the east trench, we detected red and black coloring that unmistakably represented the feather headdress of one of the warriors depicted in the famous fresco (Fig. 30; cf. Fig. 7). This was the breakthrough we had been waiting for. The discovery thrilled us, not only because we had finally found the murals but also because some sections appeared to have survived against all expectations. Gradually, we exposed a section of the wall, taking extra precautions to shield it from the sun. We carefully uncovered an entire warrior figure, though its upper portion was unfortunately damaged by tree roots (Fig. 31). As we excavated the full trench, we discovered that the murals were not 18 meters in length, as previously believed, but rather extended to 30 meters. While the central portion had been destroyed – likely corresponding to the section looted in the past century – both extremities of the murals remained untouched, totaling 12 meters. It appears the looters did not excavate the entire wall, leaving these parts hidden and partially preserved for more than 1,000 years.

Fig. 31 Conditions were far from perfect as a root had damaged the warrior's face.

The fragile nature of the murals necessitated immediate protective measures. To prevent prolonged exposure to the open air, we created a complete photogrammetric record of the artwork before roofing the area to ensure its preservation. Additionally, we collaborated with a specialist from the Sicán Museum, under the direction of archaeologist Carlos Elera, to produce a full-scale drawing of the murals. This effort was accompanied by visits from two prominent archaeologists from Lambayeque: Carlos Wester, the director of the Brüning Museum, and Bernarda Delgado, the director of the Túcume Museum. The detailed drawing allowed us to better define the features of the warriors' faces, facilitating a complete reconstruction of each figure depicted in their respective cells. This resource will be invaluable for comparing the murals with other Moche and Lambayeque artistic styles, aiding in the interpretation of their symbolic content (Figs. 32 and 33).

Uncovering the wall on which the fresco was painted allowed us to contextualize its use and gain a deeper understanding of the architectural layout of the monument, which most likely served as a temple. The structure is composed of two main levels enclosed by a perimeter wall. The first level is a large platform capable of accommodating a significant number of attendees and is connected to the upper section by a central ramp. The second level is a raised plaza overlooking the platform, with access seemingly restricted to the protagonist of the ritual that likely took place in the

Fig. 32 A general view of the panel after uncovering gently the whole wall.

Fig. 33 Full size drawing layer with specialist César Samillán and his assistant from the Sicán Museum.

Fig. 34 General view of the excavations on top of the Huaca Pintada with the 30-meter wall completely uncovered.

space. The great painted wall and parts of the plaza were covered by a roof, perhaps resembling a patio, to shield the architecture from climatic events. As Orrego (1927) rightly observed, the structure includes several interconnected compartments forming a quadrilateral shape, open on its western side (Fig. 34). At the rear, the fresco, 30 meters long and approximately 3 meters high, depicts an intricate mythological scene of exceptional detail. This arrangement recalls the altar of a cathedral, where the priest conducts ceremonies before a richly decorated backdrop, enhancing his words while visually narrating sacred episodes. In such settings, saints adorned with halos emphasize their divine status. Similarly, the majesty of Huaca Pintada's artwork, along with the interplay of sound (echoes) and light (mosaics), evokes a profound sense of sacredness, reinforcing the myths that are at the same time performed in the rituals and illustrated by the fresco. This was likely the intended effect of such an extraordinary display.

The discovery of the fresco was particularly significant, as it was entirely unexpected to find sections that had remained untouched by looters. It represents an invaluable piece of pre-Hispanic Indigenous art from the Lambayeque region, which can now be recovered and appreciated in its authentic form. Encountering these images in their original context on the temple's upper section inspires a profound sense of monumentality and

Fig. 35 Construction of an adobe wall and filling the spaces with clean sand in order to protect the paintings.

connection to a sacred Indigenous landscape. But above all, this discovery has the potential, through a thoughtfully designed valorization initiative, to make these ancient images accessible to the local community, who are the rightful heirs to this rich tradition. Indeed, a fundamental goal of archaeological research is to return the knowledge acquired during excavations to the communities most directly linked to the findings. However, first and most importantly, we needed to ensure its preservation. After our fieldwork, we adhered to strict conservation measures mandated by the Ministry of Culture. These included covering the painted areas with a modern adobe wall, filling the spaces with clean sand, and reburying the entire section to ensure its preservation (Fig. 35).

An intriguing characteristic of Huaca Pintada is that its function shifted over time, becoming an important pre-Hispanic cemetery following its abandonment by the Lambayeque people roughly 1,000 years ago. Among the oldest funerary contexts we uncovered were the burials of two individuals from the Middle Lambayeque period, interred in the central part of the huaca shortly after it was covered by sand. Their graves included finely crafted offerings, such as a pair of iconic "Huaco Rey" vessels representing a deified ancestor. Interestingly, one Huaco Rey vessel displayed intentional mutilations on specific features, including the crown of the ancestor and the two attendants depicted on its flanks. This deliberate alteration suggests a complex ritual or specific circumstances surrounding the individual's death and burial (Figs. 36 and 37).

Fig. 36 Individual from the Middle Lambayeque period accompanied with a couple of Huaco Rey vessels.

Fig. 37 Huaco Rey vessel "mutilated" next to the second individual. What was their intention through such a practice?

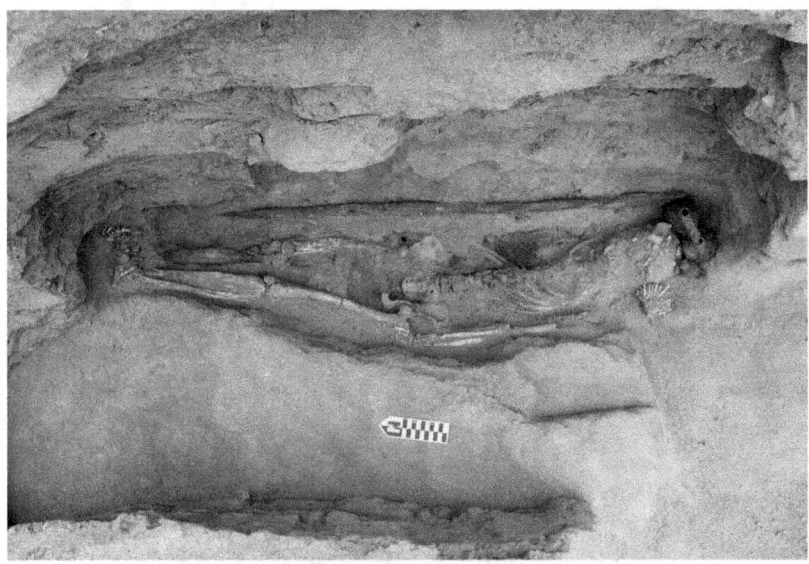

Fig. 38 Individual belonging to the Inca period buried with a wooden stick used to brew chicha.

Furthermore, we discovered the remains of more than 25 individuals from the Inca period. This finding was particularly surprising, as the Inca conquest of the north coast occurred around 500 years after the construction of the huaca. For reasons yet unclear, the monument regained its prestige during this period. The concentration of individuals of Inca affiliation is rare in the region and provides valuable insights into a pivotal episode in pre-Columbian history on the northern coast of Peru. Several of the individuals were buried with exquisite ornaments, including bronze pectorals, necklaces, and bracelets, and were often accompanied by offerings such as fine ceramics and spondylus shells. These burials also revealed societal roles. For example, one woman was buried with a wooden tool used for brewing chicha. Remarkably, this tool closely resembles one still used today by Señora Inoñán of the El Potrero restaurant, located just across the street. She continues to use this traditional tool each week to prepare chicha for her customers (Figs. 38 and 39).

The most astonishing discovery was a burial chamber belonging to an Inca elite member, located directly adjacent to the murals. The significance of this context was evident from tomb markers shaped like half-moons, which were substantially larger than those associated with other burials. The grave consisted of an antechamber containing several sacrificed human heads and an array of prestigious goods, including a golden ring. The main chamber, situated on the western side, held more than 100 artifacts spanning various materials such as

Fig. 39 Doña Tantarico brewing her chicha in the El Potrero restaurant.

ceramics, metals, wood, and shells. The primary individual's remains were disarticulated, suggesting they had been displaced and reburied at this site after decomposition, following an ancient tradition already observed within the Moche culture (Nelson and Castillo, 1997). We believe it is likely that these individuals were moved from their original burial sites to be reinterred in this new location after their death, to claim the sacred space of the temple or, more broadly, the surrounding territory. This practice allowed communities to legitimize their presence by burying their ancestors in significant locations, thereby strengthening their connection to the land. By selecting sites of particular importance to the local community, they established a sense of ancestral continuity, asserting their rights and belonging to the area. Furthermore, they may have sought to forge kinship relationships with sacred entities, emphasizing their divine origin as ancestors of the same communities they sought to dominate (Lau, 2021). The location of Huaca Pintada, situated at the border between the territories of Illimo – Batán Grande to the north and Túcume to the south – could explain this heightened interest. Thus the practice of relocating the deceased to another burial site, as seems to be the case for the individuals in

Fig. 40 Excavation of the Inca burial chamber with Nayo and Don Damian.

the burial chamber, might signify an effort to claim rights over conquered territory. This was achieved by shaping beliefs about ancestral authority through specific funerary practices.

These enigmatic funerary practices, embedded in traditional ecological knowledge, also impacted the course of our excavations. For example, when removing a vessel featuring a detailed depiction of a crawling snake, a live snake emerged from the same hole. To the members of the community working with us, this was undoubtedly a sign from the huaca warning us to proceed with caution while excavating this burial (Figs. 40 and 41).

Some ceramics in the funerary chamber were perfectly preserved, while others were shattered, possibly as part of a ritual. The discovery of golden artifacts further underscored the individual's prestigious status. Alongside the ring, we uncovered a pair of tweezers likely used for shaving and a lime pallet shaped like a hummingbird's beak. The pallet would have been used to insert a small amount of limestone into the mouth while chewing coca leaves, activating enzymes that enhance the stimulant's effects (Figs. 42, 43, and 44). This tradition is still vivid today in Peru among people who chew coca leaves.

These discoveries are valuable not only for their aesthetic significance but also for their ability to reconstruct key historical events associated with the

Fig. 41 The ceramic depicting a crawling snake next to where a real snake was hiding.

Fig. 42 Details of the ceramic offerings of the burial chamber. It is possible to recognize a parrot.

huaca. Such events have been allegorically preserved in oral tradition, notably in a local legend recorded by A. León-Baradiarán, a Lambayeque folklorist of the 20th century. Narrated in the 1930s by Doña Nicolasa Gonzáles Márquez, a member of La Pintada at that time, the legend recounts that long before the

Fig. 43 The golden lime pallet the Inca used to insert limestone while chewing coca leaves.

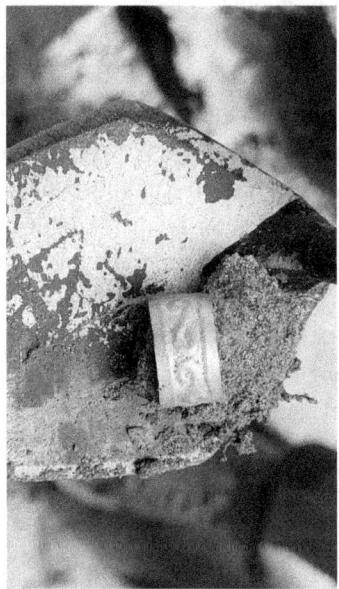

Fig. 44 The golden ring showing a subtle detail of snakelike shapes.

arrival of the Incas, a priest named Anto Tunpa resided at Huaca Pintada, dedicating his worship to the moon, rain, rivers, lizards, and spiders. One night, the sun appeared in his dream, instructing him to honor it as well.

However, the priest ignored this celestial warning, prompting the sun to burn the temple, killing the priest in the process. The legend explains that from that day onward, the walls of Huaca Pintada have been painted red, blue, and yellow – the colors of the sun, sky, and gold. These same colors remain visible on the murals today (León-Baradiarán, 1938).

What is striking is that the moon, the lizards, and the ocean are usually related to coastal deities in pre-Hispanic times. In contrast, the sun served as the central deity in the Inca imperial religion. This legend appears to metaphorically recount the Inca conquest of the north coast. In many ways, it aligns perfectly with the discovery of this unique Inca presence at Huaca Pintada.

Moreover, the legend mentions the colors of the murals, which match precisely those we uncovered at the site. This continuity suggests that knowledge of the murals remained in the collective memory of the local community for at least 500 years. Remarkably, the legend predates the 1916 discovery of the murals. Historical archives reveal that the name Huaca Pintada (The Painted Temple) has been in use since at least the mid 19th century, likely derived from the knowledge of these hidden paintings. It is even possible that the original Muchik name for the huaca carried a similar meaning in the vernacular language. We are currently examining colonial-era regional archives in search of references to unknown huacas that may align with this description.

At the end of the 2022 field season, we shared traditional *chancho al palo* (grilled pork) with our team and the community members who had supported us throughout the years. The final day of work is also a key moment in an excavation; it is undoubtedly a significant milestone for any archaeological project. It provides a moment of conviviality, bringing the team together after long, challenging work that often tests group cohesion. For a project leader, expressing gratitude to the team whose efforts made such results possible is essential. In this sense, hosting an end-of-field-season gathering becomes an act of reciprocity that aligns with the values of La Pintada community. Much like the preparation and sharing of chicha, this practice seeks to strengthen personal relations while challenging conventional hierarchies in the fieldwork. It insists on a participatory and reciprocal process, transforming archaeological work into a shared moment with the community. In this context, the conclusion of an excavation, marked by a communal gathering, exemplifies these principles. Such gatherings are not merely celebratory but serve as an intentional practice of relational accountability, acknowledging the collective efforts of the team and the community while honoring the shared connection to the site (Smith, 1999).

The visit of Don Augusto Granados and Professor Inoñán's heartfelt reaction to the murals further illustrate how relationality extends to knowledge-sharing

Fig. 45 End-of-project party with the visit of Don Augusto Granados during the whole day.

and emotional resonance. Professor Inoñán's reflection – "I will need no photo; these images are now etched in my mind forever" – highlights how the application of those methodologies engages not only intellectual understanding but also emotional and spiritual connections. By foregrounding Indigenous relationality, the project becomes more than an academic pursuit; it evolves into a practice that respects and revitalizes the ties between people, history, and place (Figs. 45 and 46).

Once fieldwork concluded, we sought funding to support future projects aimed at valorizing the Huaca Pintada site. Media coverage of our discoveries helped us secure a special grant from the Swiss-Liechtenstein Foundation for Archaeological Research Abroad (SLSA). This funding enables us to restore and conserve the artifacts uncovered in the Inca burial chamber. This project holds immense potential. First, it will advance archaeological and historical research, as analyzing the offering sets can shed light on the funerary practices of noble families in this region during a period of intense cultural interaction. The diversity of this material contributes significantly to the study of pre-Columbian cultures on Peru's northern coast and the demographic changes brought about by the Inca conquest at the end of the 15th century AD, just decades before Pizarro's arrival in search of El Dorado. Furthermore, this

Fig. 46 Don Damian, Luigui, Nayo, and Lucho having a laugh with Sebastian, the son of Milagros.

project offers an opportunity to restore the splendor of these ancient artifacts, which have shaped the cultural identity of these communities for centuries (Figs. 47 and 48).

Following the analysis of the archaeological artifacts, this project could lead to the organization of temporary exhibitions in museums in both Peru and Switzerland. Carlos Wester La Torre, the director of the Brüning Archaeological Museum in Lambayeque, has already expressed interest in showcasing these findings in their exhibition spaces once operations are complete. This would be a significant achievement, allowing local communities to finally engage with these fascinating relics of their past and ensuring that the new knowledge gleaned from Huaca Pintada is passed on to future generations.

Our team, composed of students from the Pedro Ruiz Gallo University of Lambayeque, is currently working on this delicate material in the laboratories of

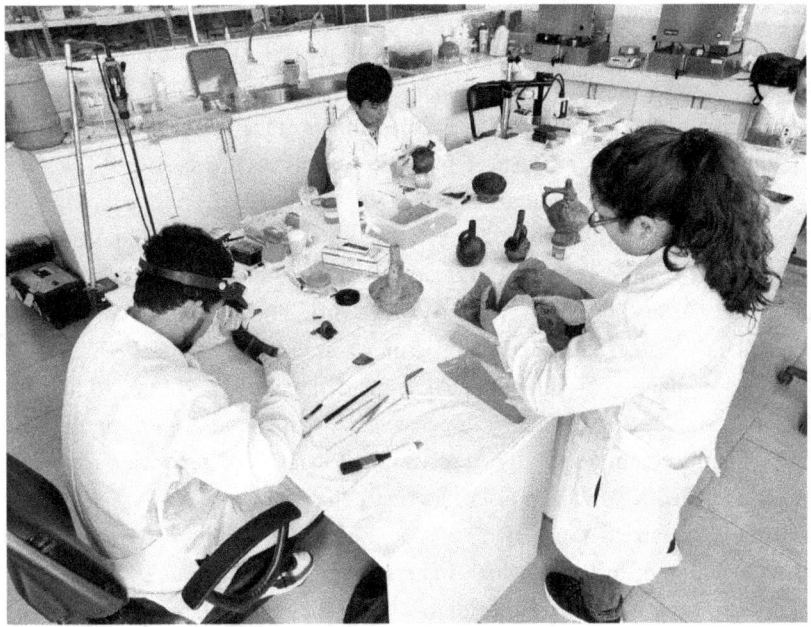

Fig. 47 Jhordan, Javier, and Maria, who collaborated with us in the field, working in the lab of the Brüning Museum on the restauration of the archaeological artefacts we discovered in 2022.

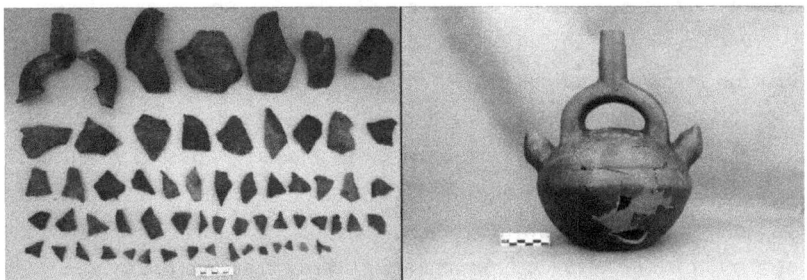

Fig. 48 A typical bottle of the Chimú–Inca style of the north coast of Peru, before and after restoration.

the Brüning Museum under the supervision of the institution's chief conservator. This experience provides an invaluable educational opportunity for these students and represents the first step in a larger preservation project to be developed over the next few years in collaboration with the community. This initiative will not only deepen our understanding of the history of Huaca Pintada but also raise awareness among local authorities about the importance of preserving the site. Furthermore, it aims to promote the safeguarding and development of local heritage, which is frequently threatened by the illicit looting of archaeological sites in the region.

In this spirit, we held discussions with members of the local community about the site's significance and the need for collective efforts to preserve it. Together, we agreed that, once the murals can be safely exposed to the public through the construction of a protective roof, a system of rotating guards would need to be organized to ensure their security. Additionally, Ronald Granados suggested that once the restoration of artifacts at the Brüning Museum is complete, it would be ideal to establish a small site museum in the village of La Pintada to house the findings. This initiative, aligned with the directives of the Ministry of Culture, could serve as a model of co-ownership of archaeological heritage by involving the community in its preservation. It would also generate jobs related to the maintenance and care of the site's structures.

Another recurring topic of discussion was the possibility of restoring the central section of the wall, which looters destroyed more than 100 years ago. This idea contrasts with the traditional archaeological focus on preserving remains in their found state, emphasizing an almost obsessive commitment to the authenticity of material artifacts. In contrast, the community of La Pintada takes pride in the vibrant colors that once adorned the walls of their huaca and envisions the reconstruction of the wall as a way to celebrate their heritage. Such a restoration, while highlighting the contrast between original and reconstructed sections, could be guided by the detailed photographs taken by Heinrich Brüning before the wall's destruction, which provide an accurate depiction of the original images.

Restoring the mural would also enhance the accessibility of the site, creating an opportunity for visitors to experience the impressive fresco, which is 30 meters long, nearly 3 meters high, and composed of at least five distinct colors. The monumentality of this work is unparalleled in the region and would attract not only tourists but also local residents with deep connections to this land. Such a project could empower the community by strengthening its historical identity, boosting the local economy, and sustaining the archaeological project by fostering continued interest in the site's investigation and preservation in the years to come.

In March 2023, our collaboration proved invaluable during an unforeseen and critical event. The powerful Yaku cyclone inundated the Lambayeque region with torrential rains for an entire month, causing severe flooding of major rivers. Many families, caught off guard by the rapid onset of the cyclone, lost their homes and were forced to seek refuge with friends or in classrooms converted into temporary shelters, significantly disrupting their daily lives. Fortunately,

Fig. 49 Jhordan and Javier preparing the baskets of essential foods during the Yaku cyclone that flooded the Lambayeque region in early 2023.

the flooding of the La Leche River did not reach La Pintada, but we still took proactive measures to protect the areas where the murals are located. This included installing large tarpaulins to prevent water infiltration and pumping stagnant water off the huaca daily.

We recognized that moments like these required us to assist the community in navigating such challenges. To this end, we organized a fundraiser to support the affected families of La Pintada. With the collected funds, we purchased essential food items and distributed baskets to those in need. Additionally, we assessed the most impacted homes and provided materials such as metal sheets and other necessities to aid in their recovery (Figs. 49, 50, and 51).

We also allocated resources to make a donation to the Liceo Aguirre La Pintada, located adjacent to the huaca. This school is a vital space for educating the younger generation, and we share the belief that cultural institutions must invest in the future of children. Despite the difficulties faced, it was crucial that the school's work continue under proper conditions, as it symbolizes the heart of the La Pintada community. Through this donation, we aimed to reaffirm our commitment to the community and express our willingness to support its development. The donations included shelves, educational books on Peruvian

Fig. 50 Professor Vidal Cobeñas receiving the donation of a basket from Mateo, Maricela's son.

history, and various school supplies. Professor Inoñán organized a ceremony on the day celebrating the Peruvian flag to acknowledge this contribution and later sent us a letter of thanks, which is included in this document with his consent (Figs. 52, 53, 54, and 55).

4 Archaeological Sites as Indigenous Anchors in the Landscape

In the Andean territory, multiple ways of seeing and being are articulated, with a long-standing interrelation between communities and the land embedded within the concept of the sacred landscape. However, colonialism and so-called modernity have gradually disconnected people from what were once the most important sacred spaces in the Andean area: the huacas. Ancient Peruvians believed that rocks, rivers, mountains, springs, and all the elements that make up the landscape were living entities, a belief shared across many Indigenous communities (Dongoske, 2020). These entities hold attributes of

Fig. 51 Distribution of metal sheets and plastics tarps for the community of La Pintada.

sacredness, understood as huacas or deities, which possess great communication power and actively influence people's lives. In other words, "the huacas truly speak" (Curatola 2016) (Fig. 56).

Ceremonial centers, shrines, and settlements also acquired the status of huaca because they are integrated within the sacred landscape. Apparently, the Incas took this perspective to the extreme, as their expansion would have had not only sociopolitical characteristics but also religious ones, seeking to replicate their sacred landscape, Cusco, in their provinces (Makowski, 2015). From this perspective, the control of powerful huacas would also have been a strategy of power, a phenomenon that aligns with our recent findings at Huaca Pintada. On the other hand, there are other symbolic qualities of archaeological sites that would be worth exploring to approach the Indigenous knowledge we are referring to.

Fig. 52 Shelves with educational books donated to the Liceo Aguirre La Pintada.

Fig. 53 Luigui Oliva from the PIAHP posing with Professor Vidal during the donation ceremony.

Fig. 54 All the students of the Liceo Aguirre La Pintada were present that day.

For example, Allen's work on earthworks explores why human groups chose to build mounds, embankments, etcetera, assessing the motivations behind the construction itself and delving into the realm of "experiences" (attitudes of perception). These range from organization of labor to the creation of constructed spaces (Allen, 2021). What would the native populations have felt when they built Huaca Pintada? Clearly this is a topic not extensively explored by researchers, as the voice of native communities is often excluded from our reconstructions, missing the opportunity to experiment with alternative approaches to materiality. Allen (2021, p. 216) suggests that earthworks constitute Indigenous knowledge in themselves and are a form of Indigenous "writing." However, their "reading" does not involve abstract codified drawings but rather bodily and performative methodologies. In this line of thought, huacas could be seen as embodied and animated materiality containing social, psychic, and spiritual power – an encounter between humans and nonhumans.

Another quality of huacas, from a social perspective, is that they would act as mechanisms of integration and social reproduction. In pre-Hispanic Andean cultures, writing was unknown, so effective ways of transmitting social memory were necessary since it did not operate in the abstract. In other words, the ceremonial centers or huacas acted as anchors that tied the social memory to the land, making it not only visible but also tangible. Excavations at various archaeological complexes in the Andean region have revealed that these monuments underwent constant remodeling, additions, overlays, seals, offerings, etcetera. As these repetitions occurred, social norms were constantly recreated.

Fig. 55 The letter of thanks from Professor Vidal Cobeñas after the donations.

Additionally, these centers facilitated the interaction of different communities, exchanging not only material but also knowledge. The case of Huaca Pintada is exceptional, understood as a landmark since it is located on the boundary between two local groups tied to their land – the Illimo and Tucume peoples – both with shared social memory but with clearly differentiated elements.

As argued, huacas are active entities, bridges of communion with the land, and spaces of communication between human and nonhuman entities. This relational perspective has become increasingly relevant in the growing body of literature on

Fig. 56 Tupa Inca talking to the huacas in the chronicle of Guaman Póma de Ayala (2005 [1615], p. 261).

traditional ecological knowledge (TEK) (Allen, 2021; Dudgeon, 2021; Inglis, 1993; Lozada and Tantalean, 2019; Lyons and Supernant, 2020; Menzies, 2006; Pierotti and Wildcat, 2000). In modern Western logic, the landscape is reduced to a resource to be dominated and exploited, whereas in the TEK of local communities, there is a codependence and conditions for mutual respect in the sense that the land not only provides resources but also teaches good living and a morality for the collective benefit. However, many variables have been consolidated in modernity, including the state itself, economic interests, tourism, "the cultural," etcetera (including protected areas), affecting the true custodians of the landscapes, the local communities, who might even lose legal access to ancient ceremonial centers.

Here, a dichotomy arises that needs exploration, as while the land is the community's most valuable resource, it is also a source of latent insecurity: the danger of losing their landscape due to conservation policies derived from national and international agendas under labels like "cultural heritage." Consequently, there is a constant need to defend the community's rights.

State policies often use an "epistemology of crisis," which involves quick responses and sometimes justifies violent actions such as evictions or the imposition of cultural categories that do not align with local perspectives. In contrast, the "epistemology of coordination," based on Indigenous traditions, views change as something normal and constant, managed through ethical and cooperative relationships without resorting to violence (White, 2021). This epistemology seeks to understand the world from a "relational" perspective with multidimensional and reciprocal connections. Furthermore, an epistemology of coordination would provide a collective response to problems and reinforce kinship ties that, as we have seen, extend beyond humans. For example, archaeological literature shows how huacas, as living entities, could also establish kinship, bringing about new and complex forms of relationships between interacting human groups (e.g., Pachacámac, Puruchuco, etc.). This led to the creation of new explanatory narratives that sought to legitimize the emergence of new identities resulting from these relationships.

It could be said that identities are not permanent; that is, they are created and recreated based on their degree and nature of participation in society (Singh, 2018). This allows for a rethinking of the concept of Indigenous and transcending a substantialist perspective based on the pristine, original, etcetera, toward a constructivist perspective of "being over time" more sensitive to changes. The inhabitants living around Huaca Pintada consider themselves natives of the land, although colonialism has caused movement and displacement. In this sense, we aim to overcome the presentism determined by modernity and instead search historically for local knowledge to rescue, preserve, and include it in academic discussions as alternative ways of seeing and being.

In this line of thought, while the concept of the huaca has evolved since pre-Hispanic times, continuities can also be traced, with this term remaining the most common to refer to archaeological monuments. Huacas are commonly highly respected by local populations, redefining them as places of "the ancients," "the grandparents," and ancestors: in other words, the anchors of social memory. However, pieces of information remain buried within the monuments, and unearthing them demands great responsibility and ethical commitment. This is the case with our research project at Huaca Pintada, which aims to recover these pieces of historical information and return them to their rightful owners. Therefore we consider it of utmost importance to connect archaeology and community in a modern context, not only to safeguard archaeological monuments but also to contribute to the creation of a local identity, where the past serves to shape the present and project a future (Bria and Carranza, 2015; Mellet, 2010; Rosado, 2021).

Undoubtedly, some of the most significant actors in our study community are the local teachers, as they help spread the field-recovered data among their students, which encompass not only material aspects but also symbolic and moral ones. In this sense, an increasing number of individuals identify with a past that is no longer so distant, as it is recreated in their own lives, regardless of their parents' origins. Teaching children and young people who will one day be adults to cherish Huaca Pintada is a great strategy to preserve the social memory, as they reproduce the values structured through practice, a practice that does not disconnect rationality from emotions (Lyons and Supernant, 2020). This is based on the concept that *you do not protect what you do not cherish, and you do not cherish what you do not know.* Therein lies our strength, that of contributing to forge "an identity born of diversity," taking into account that "identity is the most plural attribute of the human being" (Mellet, 2010). The Incas, not being local to La Pintada, made a local landscape their own and sacralized it, creating both material and ideological syncretic structures in the process.

Therefore we believe in an archaeology that engages with the present rather than being stuck in the past (Wobst, 2010) – that is, an archaeology that can harmonize the history of the monument within the current context. Initially, it was mentioned that the power of the huacas was based on their ability to speak. Huaca Pintada has remained mute for a long time and in the process has been losing its power. However, archaeologists can serve as a new vehicle through which the huacas communicate, preserving a connection that has endured for millennia. Thus we have already initiated different strategies that have been effective, such as conferences, workshops, and participation in the excavation itself. The first tourists have always been the members of the community, who are very interested in reconnecting their links with the monument.

5 Conclusions

Huaca Pintada is undoubtedly one of the most representative archaeological monuments on the northern coast of Peru, seamlessly connecting key historical episodes of the Andean region. It is associated with the restructuring of societies such as the Moche, the emergence of the Lambayeque peoples, and the expansion of the Inca Empire. However, its history does not end there, as the local native communities consider the huaca as the heritage of their ancestors. Therefore, it is not an anachronistic monument but a highly symbolic element within the cultural landscape. Today, social memory has weakened among the new generations due to modernity and capitalism, causing the huaca, as a living entity, to "lose its ability to speak," a key attribute within Indigenous ontology, leaving it somewhat dormant.

The Huaca Pintada Archaeological Research Project, through a collaborative approach, successfully intervened in a highly representative monument for the Andean area, but one that was difficult to access due to a disconnection between state policies, colonial perspectives, and the dispossession of ancestral lands from local communities under the label of national heritage. Thus the recovery of the monument was contemplated not only in its material dimension but also in its social dimension, seeking to rescue the cultural history of the archaeological site about its environment, including both the landscape and the community. The strengths of this project lie in its way of integrating the local population into the research in various ways including excavation, dissemination, conservation, and exhibition.

This dynamic interaction between academia, science, and Indigenous communities opens avenues for future research that must be approached with sensitivity, mutual respect, and collaboration. In our case study, the solution to resolve the initial conflict of accessibility and research came from the community itself. Additionally, the findings helped reinforce links with the past and reestablish identities that, in some way, acquire meaning in the cultural practices of those who today call themselves the guardians of the site. From a practical standpoint, the archaeological findings create educational, artisanal, commercial, and tourism opportunities that empower the community.

We consider this work not as something finite but as a project that seeks to rescue and build identity within a process involving a constant commitment to working with the community. Undoubtedly, one of the greatest achievements is having reached the local school, where an unearthed history and Indigenous knowledge are happily reproduced among children and young people, who are the key to the future. Therefore, the Indigeneity we refer to does not appeal to a pristine and static origin but rather to something that is built over time. Remarkably, despite the contingencies of modernity, oral histories and deep-rooted traditions persist, having withstood the test of time (Denisson, 2021; León-Barandiarán, 1938).

It should be emphasized that academic narratives are not more important than the narratives the community itself creates around the huaca in light of the material evidence we provide them. In this regard, we consider that the sections of history we recover should be returned to their true owners, the Indigenous peoples, as the implications of this work extend beyond purely academic and scientific research. Similarly, the true value of archaeological work lies not only in the discoveries for their aesthetic and historical values but also in what it can significantly contribute to the Indigenous communities it affects. This process involves respectful engagement and trusting relationships with Indigenous communities, ensuring that research results are accessible and beneficial to them. This could involve digital technologies, community-led educational programs, or collaborations with artists and storytellers to seek the preservation or reinterpretation of the oral tradition that tends to disappear among the new generations.

This may be the beginning of an archaeology that, instead of imposing its interpretations, works with the community to address new narratives, meanings, and knowledge beyond the understanding of the phenomena studied if observed solely through conventional scientific approaches. By interacting with Indigenous knowledge holders, researchers can enrich their understanding and develop a more nuanced perspective of cultural heritage.

Finally, we consider that reconnecting with the huaca truly means cherishing it, and for that, it is necessary to investigate it, as one cannot love and cherish something or someone they do not know. This is how our project contributes to enabling Huaca Pintada to speak again.

References

Alderman, J. (2021). House personhood in rural Andean Bolivia. *ANUAC*, 10(2), 129–154.

Allen, C. (2021). Vital earth/vibrant earthworks/living earthworks vocabularies. In B. Hokowhitu, A. Moreton-Robinson, L. Tuhiwai-Smith, C. Andersen, and S. Larkin, eds. *Routledge Handbook of Critical Indigenous Studies*. Routledge International Handbooks. London: Routledge, pp. 215–228.

Alva, W. (1994). *Sipán: Descubrimientos e investigaciones*. Colección Cultura y Artes del Perú. Lima: Backus y Johnston S. A. A.

Alva, W., and Donnan, C. B. (1993). *Royal Tombs of Sipán*. Los Angeles, CA: Fowler Museum of Cultural History, University of California, Los Angeles.

Anaya, J. (2014). *Report of the Special Rapporteur on the Rights of Indigenous Peoples: The Situation of Indigenous Peoples' Rights in Peru with Regard to the Extractive Industries. Human Rights Council: Twenty-Seventh Session. United Nations General Assembly*. New York: United Nations.

Arksey, M., Peterson, M., and Pierce, G. (2020). Targeting your audience: Tailoring avocational and youth-oriented public archaeology programs for rural populations. *Advances in Archaeological Practice*, 8(4), 409–419.

Atalay, S. (2010). Indigenous archaeology as decolonizing practice. In M. M. Bruchac, S. M. Hart, and H. M. Wobst, eds. *Indigenous Archaeologies: A Reader on Decolonization*. London: Routledge, pp. 79–86.

Bauer, B. (1998). *The Sacred Landscape of the Inca: The Cusco Ceque System*. Austin: University of Texas Press.

Bawden, G. (1996). *The Moche*. Oxford: Blackwell.

Bennett, W. C. (1939). *Archaeology of the North Coast of Peru: An Account of Exploration and Excavation in Viru and Lambayeque Valleys*. Anthropological Papers of the American Museum of Natural History, Volume XXXVII, Part 1. New York: The American Museum of Natural History.

Bohn, A., Kiggen, M. H. H., Uthaug, M. V., van Oorsouw, K. I. M., Ramaekers, J. G., and van Schie, H. T. (2022). Altered states of consciousness during ceremonial San Pedro use. *International Journal for the Psychology of Religion*, 33(4), 309–331.

Bonavía, D. (1985). *Mural Painting in Ancient Peru*. Translated by Patricia J. Lyon. Bloomington: Indiana University Press.

Bria, R., and Carranza, E. (2015). Making the past relevant: Co-creative approaches to heritage preservation and community development at Hualcayán, Ancash, Peru. *Advances in Archaeological Practice*, 3(3), 208–222.

Brüning, H. H. (1917). Provincia de Lambayeque: Contribución arqueológica. *Boletín de la Sociedad Geográfica de Lima*, 32, 197–201.

Castillo, L. J. (2012). San José de Moro y el Fin de los Mochicas en el Valle de Jequetepeque, Costa Norte del Perú. Dissertation submitted in partial satisfaction of the requirements for the degree of doctor of philosophy in anthropology. Los Angeles: University of California.

Castillo Butters, L. J. (2001). The last of the Mochicas: A view from the Jequetepeque valley. In J. Pillsbury, ed. *Moche Art and Archaeology in Ancient Peru*. Studies in the History of Art 63. Center for Advanced Studies in the Visual Arts, Symposium Papers XL. Washington, DC: National Gallery of Art, pp. 307–332.

Chirinos Ogata, P. (2018). Entre tumbas y medianoche: Contextos y cambios de las representaciones sobre los "huaqueros" en el Perú. *Cuadernos CANELA*, 29, 37–55.

Cojti Ren A. (2010). Maya archaeology and the political and cultural identity of contemporary Maya in Guatemala. In M. M. Bruchac, S. M. Hart, and H. M. Wobst, eds. *Indigenous Archaeologies: A Reader on Decolonization*. London: Routledge, pp. 203–210.

Conkey, M. W. (2010). Dwelling at the margins, action at the 91 intersection? Feminist and Indigenous archaeologies, 2005. In M. M. Bruchac, S. M. Hart, and H. M. Wobst, eds. *Indigenous Archaeologies: A Reader on Decolonization*. London: Routledge, pp. 1–98.

Curatola Petrocchi, M. (2016). La voz de la huaca: Acerca de la naturaleza oracular y el trasfondo aural de la religión andina antigua. In M. Curatola Petrocchi and J. Szemiński, eds. *El Inca y la Huaca: La Religión del Poder y el Poder de la Religión en el Mundo Andino Antiguo*. Lima: Fondo Editorial de la Pontificia Universidad Católica del Perú, pp. 259–316.

Curo Chambergo, M., and Rosas Fernández, J. (2014). Complejo Arqueológico Huaca Bandera Pacora: Un sitio transicional Moche – Lambayeque. In J. C. Fernández Alvarado and C. E. Wester La Torre, eds. *Cultura Lambayeque, en el contexto de la costa norte del Perú: Actas del primer y segundo coloquio*. Chiclayo: EMDECOSEGE, pp. 245–270.

Cusicanqui Marsano, S. (2023). Construyendo memoria y comunidad. In Agencia Española de Cooperación Internacional para el Desarrollo, ed., *Escuela Taller Perú 30 años: "Aprender Haciendo."* Lima: Agencia Española de Cooperación Internacional para el Desarrollo, pp. 6–99.

Dennison, J. (2021). Relational accountability in Indigenous governance: Navigating the doctrine of distrust in the Osage Nation. In B. Hokowhitu, A. Moreton-Robinson, L. Tuhiwai Smith, C. Andersen, and S. Larkin, eds.

Routledge Handbook of Critical Indigenous Studies. London: Routledge, pp. 295–309.

Dongoske, K. (2020). Making mitigation meaningful to descendant communities: An example from Zuni. *Advances in Archaeological Practice,* 8(3), 225–235.

Doughty, C. (2014). Examining participation and power between local actors in the Peruvian Andes: Andean Ecosystem Association and the Indigenous communities of the Vilcanota. *Tropical Resources Bulletin,* 32–33, 24–30.

Dube, R. (2014). Peru's modern economy clashes with its past. *The Wall Street Journal,* September 10. www.wsj.com/articles/development-in-peru-clashes-with-its-ancient-past-1410397160.

Dudgeon, P. (2021). Decolonising psychology: Self-determination and social and emotional wellbeing. In B. Hokowhitu, A. Moreton-Robinson, L. Tuhiwai-Smith, C. Andersen, and S, Larkin, eds. *The Routledge Handbook of Critical Indigenous Studies.* 1st ed. New York: Routledge, pp. 100–113.

Favaron, P. (2017). *Las visiones y los mundos: Sendas visionarias de la Amazonia occidental.* Lima: Universidad Nacional de Ucayali and Centro Amazónico de Antropología y Aplicación Práctica.

Fernández Manayalle, M. A. (2016). *Asentamientos Transicionales en el territorio de la Cultura Lambayeque.* Chiclayo: Ministerio de Cultura del Perú, Unidad Ejecutora 005, Proyecto Especial Naylamp Lambayeque.

Gareis, I. (2007). Extirpación de idolatrías e identidad cultural en las sociedades andinas del Perú virreinal (siglo XVII). *Nuevo Mundo Mundos Nuevos.* Bibliothèque des Auteurs du Centre.

Ghavami, S. (2021). Entre Mochica et Lambayeque: Retracer les identités de la période Transitionnelle dans les empreintes du quotidien. *Journal de la Société des Américanistes,* 107(1), 45–76.

Guamán Poma de Ayala, F. (2005) [1615]. *Nueva Corónica y BuenGobierno.* Edited by F. Pease. Lima: Editorial Fondo de Cultura Económica.

Hall, M. (2001). Cape Town's District Six and the archaeology of memory. In R. Layton, P. Stone, and J. Thomas, eds. *Destruction and Conservation of the Cultural Property.* One World Archaeology 41. London: Routledge, pp. 298–311.

Hepfer, T. (2017). *Das Gräberfeld von Illimo – Nordperu.* A thesis submitted in partial satisfaction of the requirements for the degree of master of arts in anthropology. Hamburg University, Germany.

Heyerdahl, T. (1950). *Kon-Tiki: Across the Pacific by Raft.* Chicago, IL: Rand McNally.

Heyerdahl, T., Sandweiss D. H., and Narváez A. (1995). *Pyramids of Túcume: The Quest for Peru's Forgotten City.* London: Thames and Hudson.

Huambachano, M., and Cooper, L. (2020). Values, knowledge, and rights shaping land use in the Peruvian Amazon: The Shimaa and Diamante case studies. *Case Studies in the Environment* 4(1), 1234945. https://doi.org/10.1525/cse.2020.1234945.1.

Inglis, J. (ed.) (1993). *Traditional Ecological Knowledge: Concepts and Cases*. Ottawa: International Development Research Centre.

Jessen, B., Smith, A., and Turner, C. (2022). Contributions of Indigenous knowledge to ecological and evolutionary understanding. *Frontiers in Ecology and the Environment*, 20(2), 93–101.

Joralemon, D. (1985). Altar symbolism in Peruvian ritual healing. *Journal of Latin American Lore*, 11(1), 3–29.

Kania, M. (2019). *Indigenous Peoples' Rights and Cultural Heritage: Threats and Challenges for a New Model of Heritage Policy*. London: Routledge.

Kosiba, S. (2015). Tracing the Inca past: Ritual movement and social memory in the Inca imperial capital. In M. Barnes, I. de Castro, J. Flores Espinoza, D. Kurella, and K. Noack, eds. *Perspectives on the Inca*. Stuttgart: Linden-Museum, Sonderband/Tribus, pp. 178–205.

Larco, R. (1948). *Cronología arqueológica del norte del Perú*. Buenos Aires: Bibliothèque du Musée d'Archéologie Rafael Larco Herrera, Hacienda Chiclin. Sociedad Geográfica Americana.

Lau, G. F. (2021). Animating idolatry: Making ancestral kin and personhood in ancient Peru. *Religions*, 12(5), 287–304.

Lavalle, J. A. (1989). *Culturas Precolombinas: Lambayeque*. Colección Arte y Tesoros del Perú. Lima: Banco de Crédito del Perú.

Leitão, J. (2014). *The Book of St. Cyprian: The Sorcerer's Treasure*. Keighley: Hadean Press.

León-Barandiarán, A. D. (1938). *Mitos leyendas y Tradiciones Lambayecanas*. Lima: Club de autores y lectores.

Lozada, M. C., and Tantaleán, H. (eds.) (2019). *Andean Ontologies: New Archaeological Perspectives*. Gainesville: University Press of Florida.

Lyons, N., and Supernant, K. (2020). Introduction to an archaeology of the heart. In K. Supernatant, J. Baxter, N. Lyons, and S. Atalay, eds. *Archaeologies of the Heart*. Cham: Springer Nature Switzerland, pp. 1–19.

Mackey, C. J., and Pillsbury, J. (2013). Cosmology and ritual on a Lambayeque beaker. In M. Young-Sánchez, ed. *Pre-Columbian Art & Archaeology: Essays in Honor of Frederick R. Mayer*. Papers from the 2002 and 2007 Mayer Center Symposia at the Denver Art Museum. Denver, CO: Denver Art Museum, pp. 115–141.

Makowski, K. (2016). "A game of thrones": Mecanismos de poder e identidades en la cultura material del Horizonte Medio. In M. Giersz and

K. Makowski, eds. *Nuevas Perspectivas en la Organización Política Wari.* Warsaw: Boletín del Centro de Estudios Precolombinos de la Universidad de Varsovia, pp. 31–368.

Makowski, K. (2015). Pachacamac: Old Wak'a or Inka syncretic deity? Imperial transformation of the sacred landscape in the lower Ychsma (Lurín) Valley. In T. L. Bray, ed. *The Archaeology of Wak'as: Explorations of the Sacred in the Pre-Columbian Andes.* Denver: University Press of Colorado, pp. 127–166.

Mariátegui, J. C. (1928). *Siete Ensayos de Interpretación de la Realidad Peruana.* Lima: Editorial Minerva.

Martínez Fiestas, J. (2014). El guerrero de Illimo: Un entierro Lambayeque de jerarquía media. In J. C. Fernández Alvarado and C. E. Wester La Torre, eds. *Cultura Lambayeque en el contexto de la costa norte del Perú: Actas del primer y segundo coloquio.* Chiclayo: Empresa de Desarrollo Comercial y de Servicios Generales, pp. 79–106.

Mellet, P. T. (2010). *Lenses on Cape Identities: Exploring Roots in South Africa.* Cape Town: DIBANISA.

Menzies, C. R. (2006). *Traditional Ecological Knowledge and Natural Resource Management.* Lincoln: University of Nebraska Press.

Millaire, J.-F. (2002). *Moche Burial Patterns: An Investigation into Prehispanic Social Structure.* BAR International Series 1066. Oxford: Archaeopress.

Morales, R. A. (2024). Indigeneity and territoriality in Peru: The politics of recognition and citizenship. *Cultural Survival.* www.culturalsurvival.org/news/indigeneity-and-territoriality-peru-politics-recognition-and-citizenship.

Muro Ynoñán, L. A. (2023). Moche deathscapes: Performance, politics, and the creation of myth in Huaca La Capilla–San José de Moro (AD 650–740). *Journal of Social Archaeology*, 23(3), 243–263.

Narváez Vargas, A. (2014). *Dioses, Encantos y Gentiles: Introducción al Estudio de la Tradición Oral Lambayecana.* Chiclayo: Unidad Ejecutora 005 Naylamp Lambayeque, Ministerio de Cultura.

Nelson, A., and Castillo, L. J. (1997). Huesos a la deriva: Taphonomie et traitement funéraire dans les enterrements Mochica tardifs de San José de Moro. *Boletín de Arqueología de la PUCP*, 1, 137–163.

Orrego, L. (1927). La Huaca Pintada: Su antigüedad y origen probable. Su importancia como fuente histórica. In R. A. Miranda Romero, ed. *Monografía general del departamento de Lambayeque.* Chiclayo: Talleres Tipográficos El Tiempo, pp. CCXXXV–CCXXXVI.

Pease, F. (2007). *Los Incas.* Lima: Fondo Editorial PUCP.

Pierotti, R., and Wildcat, D. (2000). Traditional ecological knowledge: The third alternative (commentary). *Ecological Applications*, 10(5), 1333–1340.

Rick, J. (2015). Religión y autoridad en Chavín de Huántar. In P. Fux, ed. *Chavín*. Lima: Museo de Arte de Lima (MALI), pp. 176–184.

Rosado, R. (2021). Living with Ruins: Community Regeneration after Political Collapse at the Ancient Maya City of Ake, Yucatán, Mexico. PhD thesis. Northwestern University.

Rucabado-Yong, J. (2006). Elite Mortuary Practices at San José de Moro during the Transitional Period: The Case Study of Collective Burial M-U615. A thesis submitted in partial satisfaction of the requirements for the degree of master of arts in anthropology. University of North Carolina at Chapel Hill.

Rucabado-Yong, J., and Castillo, L. J. (2003). El Periodo Transicional en San José de Moro. In S. Uceda and E. Mujica, eds. *Moche Hacia el Final del Milenio: Actas del Segundo Coloquio sobre la Cultura Moche. Vol. 1*. Lima: Universidad Nacional de Trujillo y Pontificia Universidad Católica del Perú, pp. 15–42.

Rødal, L. M. (2017). Fear and looting in Peru. *Nicolay: Arkeologisk Tidsskrift*, 130(1), 8–13.

SAFE (Saving Antiquities for Everyone) (2018). Cultural heritage at risk: Peru. *Smarthistory*. January 11. https://smarthistory.org/cultural-heritage-risk-peru.

Schaedel, R. P. (1978). The Huaca Pintada of Illimo. *Archaeology*, 31(1), 27–37.

Shanks, M., and Tilley, C. (2016). *Re-constructing Archaeology: Theory and Practice*. London: Routledge.

Sharon, D. (1978). *Wizard of the Four Winds: A Shaman's Story*. New York: Free Press.

Shimada, I. (1994). *Pampa Grande and the Mochica Culture*. Austin: University of Texas Press.

Shimada, I. (1995). *Cultura Sicán: Dios, riqueza y poder en la costa norte del Perú*. Lima: Fundación del Banco Continental para el fomento de la educación y la cultura, EDUBANCO.

Sillar, B. (2012). *Patrimoine vivant*: The irreplaceable *illa*s and *conopa*s of Andean households. *Techniques & Culture*, 58, 66–81. https://doi.org/10.4000/tc.6247.

Singh, P. (2018). Global configurations of Indigenous identities, movements and pathways. *Thesis Eleven*, 145(1), 10–27.

Small, S. E. (2001). Shamanism and hegemony: A Gramscian approach to the Chavín Staff God. *Kroeber Anthropological Society Papers*, 85(5), 68–90.

Smith, L. T. (1999). *Decolonizing Methodologies: Research and Indigenous Peoples*. 1st ed. London: Zed Books.

Soto Roland, F. J. (2014). El negocio de la muerte: Los huaqueros y el saqueo del pasado, *La Razón Histórica*, no. 25, pp. 161–173.

Swanson, S. (2009). Repatriating cultural property: The dispute between Yale and Peru over the treasures of Machu Picchu. *San Diego International Law Journal*, 10(469), 469–496.

Uceda, S. (2010). Théocratie et sécularisme: Relations entre le temple, le noyau urbain et le changement politique aux Huacas de Moche. In J. Quilter and L. J. Castillo, eds. *New Perspectives on Moche Political Organization*. Washington, DC: Dumbarton Oaks, pp. 132–158.

Uribe-Chinen, C. (2024). The thrive for a new heritage ethos in Peru? The Qhapaq Ñan's policymaking and the ethics of community participation. *International Journal of Cultural Property*, 31(3), 278–298. www.cambridge.org/core/product/DCF97EFE08FF327B0883A68CD197783B.

Urteaga, H. H. (1917). Antiguas tradiciones del valle de Lambayeque. Los Yungas prehistóricos, las famosas dinastías, los cantares épicos, conquistas legendarias, los HIjos del Sol. La historia, el mito y la leyenda: Lima. *Variedades* 13(462), 449–451.

Viveiros de Castro, E. (2007). La forêt de miroirs: Quelques notes sur l'ontologie des esprits amazoniens. In F. Laugrand and J. G. Oosten, eds. *La nature des esprits dans les cosmologies autochtones*. Quebec: Les Presses de l'Université Laval, pp. 45–74.

Wester La Torre, C. E. (2010). *Chotuna-Chornancap: Templos, rituales y ancestros Lambayeque*. Lima: Editorial Súper Gráfica, E.I.R.L.

Wester La Torre, C. E. (2018). *Personajes de Elite en Chornancap: Una nueva visión de la cultura Lambayeque*. Chiclayo: Unidad Ejecutora N°005, Miniesterio de Cultura, Proyecto Especial Naylamp Lambayeque.

Whyte, K. (2021). Against crisis epistemology. In B. Hokowhitu, A. Moreton-Robinson, L. Tuhiwai-Smith, C. Andersen, and S. Larkin, eds. *Routledge Handbook of Critical Indigenous Studies*. London: Routledge International Handbooks, pp. 52–64.

Wobst, H. M. (2010). Indigenous archaeologies: A worldwide perspective on human materialities and human rights. In M. M. Bruchac, S. M. Hart, and H. M. Wobst, eds. *Indigenous Archaeologies: A Reader on Decolonization*. London: Routledge, pp. 7–28.

Acknowledgments

We would like to express our gratitude to all members of the Huaca Pintada Archaeological Investigation Project (PIAHP), as well as to Carlos Wester La Torre for his invaluable support. We also extend our heartfelt thanks to the members of the Huaca Pintada community, especially those mentioned in this Element, to whom we dedicate the results of our investigation.

Cambridge Elements

Indigenous Environmental Research

Series Editors

Dina Gilio-Whitaker
California State University San Marcos

Dina Gilio-Whitaker (Colville Confederated Tribes) is a lecturer of American Indian Studies at California State University San Marcos, and an independent educator in American Indian environmental policy and other issues. She teaches courses on environmentalism and American Indians, traditional ecological knowledge, religion and philosophy, Native women's activism, American Indians and sports, and decolonization. Dina is the award-winning *As Long as Grass Grows: The Indigenous Fight for Environmental Justice* (Beacon Press, 2019). She is also an award-winning journalist, with her work appearing in *Indian Country Today*, the *Los Angeles Times*, *Time.com*, *The Boston Globe*, and many more.

Clint Carroll
University of Colorado Boulder

Clint Carroll is an Associate Professor in the Department of Ethnic Studies at the University of Colorado Boulder. A citizen of the Cherokee Nation, he works at the intersections of Indigenous studies, anthropology, and political ecology. His first book, *Roots of Our Renewal: Ethnobotany and Cherokee Environmental Governance* (University of Minnesota Press, 2015), explores how tribal natural resource managers navigate the material and structural conditions of settler colonialism, and how recent efforts in cultural revitalization inform such practices through traditional Cherokee governance and local environmental knowledge. He is an active member of the Native American and Indigenous Studies Association and the Society for Applied Anthropology. He also serves on the editorial boards for *Cultural Anthropology* and *Environment and Society*.

Joy Porter
University of Birmingham

Joy Porter is University of Birmingham 125th Anniversary Chair, Professor of Indigenous and Environmental History and Principal Investigator of the Treatied Spaces Research Group. She is the Principal Investigator for "Brightening the Covenant Chain: Revealing Cultures of Diplomacy Between the Iroquois and the British Crown" (2021–2025) and "Historic Houses Global Connections: Revisioning Two Northern Ireland Historic Houses and Estates" (2024–2027). Joy has over 65 publications, including four research monographs and three other books. She received the Wordcraft Circle of Native Writers Writer of the Year Award for *The Cambridge Companion to Native American Literature* (Cambridge University Press, 2005) and a Choice Outstanding Academic Title Award for *To be Indian: The Life of Iroquois- Seneca Arthur Caswell Parker* (Oklahoma, 2023, 2001). Her latest book is *Trauma, Primitivism and the First World War: The Making of Frank Prewett* (Bloomsbury, 2021). She was born in Derry, in the North of Ireland.

Associate Editor

Matthias Wong
National University of Singapore

Matthias Wong is Senior Tutor at the National University of Singapore and an Associate of the Treatied Spaces Research Group at the University of Birmingham. His research is in the environmental humanities, specifically in the use of digital methods to recover Indigenous presence in historical sources such as maps and treaties, and in reconnecting Indigenous collections in museums with their source communities. He co-leads the "Green Toolkit for a New Space Economy" project, which aims to widen the space sector's understanding of sustainability to include the cultural and social dimensions. His collaborators include King's Digital Lab at King's College London, The Alan Turing Institute, and Nordamerika Native Museum Zurich. His research interests are on the process of meaning-making, particularly in understanding senses of time and place, and on the repercussions of trauma and disruption. His research on early modern futurity has been published in Historical Research, and he teaches courses on cultural astronomy, public history, and digital history.

Advisory Board

Ann McGrath, *Australian National University*
Camilla Brattland, *Arctic University of Norway (UIT)*
Dalo Njera, *Mzuzu University*
Kalpana Giri, *The Regional Community Forestry Training Center for Asia and the Pacific (RECOFTC)*
Simone Athayde, *Florida International University*
Joe Bryan, *University of Colorado Boulder*
Kanyinke Sena, *Egerton University*
Kyle Powys Whyte, *University of Michigan*
Dale Turner, *University of Toronto*
Michael Hathaway, *Simon Fraser University*
Paige West, *Columbia University*
Pratik Chakrabarti, *University of Houston*
Rauna Kuokkanen, *University of Lapland*
Shannon Speed, *University of California Los Angeles*
Mike Dockry, *University of Minnesota*

About the Series

Elements in Indigenous Environmental Research offers state-of-the-art interdisciplinary analyses within the rapidly growing area of Indigenous environmental research. The series investigates how environmental issues and processes relate to Indigenous socio-economic, cultural and political dynamics.

Cambridge Elements⁼

Indigenous Environmental Research

Elements in the Series

Defending Community, Territory, and Indigenous Environmental Relations
Levi Gahman, Filiberto Penados, Cristina Coc and Shelda-Jane Smith

"Alaska" Is Not a Blank Space: Unsettling Aldo Leopold's Odyssey
Julianne Warren

Indigenous Rights to Land Versus Extractivism: The Promise and Limits of ILO Convention No. 169 in Mexico
Tamara A. Wattnem

The Rediscovery of Huaca Pintada: Why Traditional Ecological Knowledge Matters Within Archaeological Environments in Peru
Sâm Ghavami and Christian Cancho Ruiz

A full series listing is available at: www.cambridge.org/EIER

For EU product safety concerns, contact us at Calle de José Abascal, 56–1°, 28003 Madrid, Spain or eugpsr@cambridge.org.

www.ingramcontent.com/pod-product-compliance
Lightning Source LLC
LaVergne TN
LVHW011737060526
838200LV00051B/3210